UNDERSTANDING MODERN MACROECONOMICS

Resources, National Income, Employment and Unemployment, Growth and Wealth, Inflation, Government Policies, Money and Interest Rates, Deficits and Debt, International, and More

by

Peter M. Gutmann

authorHOUSE™

1663 LIBERTY DRIVE, SUITE 200
BLOOMINGTON, INDIANA 47403
(800) 839-8640
WWW.AUTHORHOUSE.COM

First published by AuthorHouse 12/16/04

ISBN: 1-4208-0864-8 (sc)

Library of Congress Control Number: 2004098274

Printed in the United States of America
Bloomington, Indiana

This book is printed on acid-free paper.

PREFACE OF "UNDERSTANDING MODERN MACROECONOMICS"

This book explains modern macroeconomics. It does not use equations, graphs, diagrams or footnotes.

The book is designed to make modern macroeconomics available to those who never had a university course in economics or who had one years ago, now little remembered. The book is non-technical. Since readers are busy, the book is purposely confined to about a hundred pages.

It seeks to combat the lack of literacy in basic macroeconomics that is all too evident among Americans.

It covers a series of important subjects: resources; national output; living standards; economic growth; employment and unemployment; money and interest rates; inflation; government; deficits and debt; international; productivity; incentives; expectations; income distribution; asset markets; business fluctuations; creative destruction; planning horizons; international convergence; and more.

New York, January 2005

Table of Contents

PREFACE OF "UNDERSTANDING MODERN MACROECO-NOMICS" v

1. RESOURCES 1

2. OUTPUT 3

3. LIVING STANDARDS 5

4. GROWTH OF RESOURCES 8

5. GROWTH OF OUTPUT 12

6. GROWTH IN LIVING STANDARDS 15

7. ACTUAL AND POTENTIAL OUTPUT 18

8. THE DETERMINATION OF ACTUAL OUTPUT 20

9. MONEY AND INTEREST RATES 30

10. INFLATION 36

11. GOVERNMENT 41

12. DEFICITS AND DEBT 46

13. INTERNATIONAL 50

14. PRODUCTIVITY 63

15. INCENTIVES 65

16. EXPECTATIONS 68

17. LAGS 71

18. WAGE/PRICE FLEXIBILITY 74

19. INDUSTRY STRUCTURE 78

20. UNCERTAINTY 82

21. INCOME DISTRIBUTION.. 85

22. ECONOMIC GROWTH 89

23. CONVERGENCE 91

24. BUSINESS FLUCTUATIONS....................................... 94

25. DEMOGRAPHICS 99

26. ASSET MARKETS 103

27. PLANNING HORIZONS 106

28. CREATIVE DESTRUCTION.. 108

29. POLICY: THE SHORT RUN AND THE LONG RUN.. 109

1. RESOURCES

Countries differ substantially in the resources available to produce output. Some have lots of resources, others not.

Usually, we use the term, "factors of production" to refer to the major categories of resources. There are five broad groups of resources. Three are the classical factors of production - land, labor and capital. Two are the modern factors of production - education and technology.

The term, "land" includes not only the actual real estate, but also known natural resources that lie beneath the land, for example, petroleum. The amount of land itself, i.e. the real estate, is almost entirely fixed, though very small amounts of land can be created, for example through reclamation from the seas with dikes. But natural resources only include those that are known to exist. So, natural resources are not a fixed quantity. Discoveries will increase natural resources. Depletion will decrease natural resources.

The discovery of major gold deposits in South Africa in the 1880's greatly increased its natural resources. The discovery of major oil deposits in Saudi Arabia in the 1930's had a similar effect. So did the discovery of oil in Libya after the Second World War. In all these countries, the factor of production, "land" grew rapidly in a relatively short period of time.

Most of the factors of production are made by man, not by nature. This is obvious for capital - the plant, the equipment, the machinery, the commercial buildings, the inventories used in the process of production and distribution, plus the stock of housing for the population. It is also obvious for the stock of technology in existence and for the stock of education incorporated in human beings. Even the labor force itself

1

is man-made. Only "land" is the result of natural causes, combined with man-made exploration. In the case of land, if the natural resources are not simply hidden, but not present at all, no amount of exploration will suffice to discover them. Israel, for example, produces no oil, despite valiant attempts to find some. But "land" also includes some pure natural resources (both positive and negative) such as temperature, rainfall, soil conditions, deserts, earthquakes, and typhoons that are essentially not changeable by man.

2. OUTPUT

Inputs are required to produce output. The inputs are the services of the factors of production – land, labor, capital, education and technology. The input from the factor, "land", includes the depletion of natural resources.

The national output may be measured by the country's gross domestic product. This includes everything that is produced within the country during a year. Gross domestic product, or GDP, is the most commonly used measure of output.

However, not all of GDP is available for national consumption, for increasing the stock of capital or for net exports. Some of it must be used to replace capital equipment that is worn out in the process of production. We call this wearing out process, depreciation. Once we subtract depreciation from GDP, we have a net, instead of a gross, measure of the country's output, called net domestic product. There is still another widely used measure of net output, called national income. This is simply net national product minus indirect taxes, such as the sales tax and excise taxes on liquor and cigarettes.

National output depends on three factors: first, the quantities of the five factors of production which are available in the country; second, the efficiency of use of these factors to produce national output; third, the degree of unemployment of the five factors of production. (We discuss the last of these in another chapter.)

The quantities of the factors of production available in a country at any time depend on the history of the country, on its endowment of natural resources and on the calendar date.

The size of the labor force, the magnitude of the stock of capital, and the amount of education incorporated in the labor force depend on history. The amount of land, including known natural resources, depends on both history and natural endowment of resources. The amount of technology depends on both the history of the country and the actual calendar date. Technology tends to be international. The technology for home computers is available now, but was not available in 1975.

National output also depends on the efficiency with which the factors of production are used. In Western type capitalist market economies, resources tend to be used fairly efficiently, so that there is limited scope to increase output by reshuffling resources. But in other types of economies, resources may be used so inefficiently that there is great scope to increase output through greater efficiency alone. For example, China under Mao used its resources so poorly – due to a poor incentive system – that output was able to expand greatly after Mao's death in 1976 simply through more efficient use of existing factors of production.

3. LIVING STANDARDS

Living standards do not depend on national output alone. They depend on national output divided by the size of the national population.

Living standards are closely related to average output per worker, i.e. national output divided by the national labor force. Output per worker, in turn, depends on the quantities of the factors of production other than labor (land, capital, education, and technology) relative to the quantity of the factor of production, labor. The greater are the average quantities of land (including natural resources), capital, education and technology relative to each worker, the greater will tend to be the average output per worker. Very often, this is called worker productivity.

Obviously, there is a big difference between the working population, or employed labor force, on the one hand, and the total population on the other. The total population includes the young, who do not work, as well as the old, who are retired, both groups supported by those in the working years who are actually at work.

The distribution of the population between those who are too young to work, those who are retired from work, and those who are in the working years depends on the demographics of the population. In some countries with rapidly growing populations, such as Bangladesh, the young are a relatively high percentage of the population. In other countries, with static or declining populations, such as Italy, the retired old are a relatively high percentage of the population. It all depends on the demographic history, the social morays, and the costs and benefits of having children.

The actual labor force depends on the labor force participation rate of those in the working years. Usually, this rate is much higher among men than among women, and higher among adults in the prime working years than among teenagers. The higher the labor force participation rate, the greater the labor force will be. In the United States, the labor force participation rate for women rose substantially during the past quarter century, while the labor force participation rate for men fell somewhat during this period.

The actual number of people working equals the total labor force minus the number unemployed. Usually, in most industrialized countries, the employed labor force equals at least 85 per cent of the total labor force. In the U.S., in the past half century, it has usually been above 90 per cent.

Often, all this is summarized by calculating the ratio of people working to those not working (due to young age, old age, failure to participate in the labor force in the working years, or failure to be employed). This ratio (those working divided by those not working) has been falling in practically all the older industrialized countries, due to the aging of the population and hence increase in the number retired, plus the negative effects of low birth rates in the past on the actual labor force..

The decline in the number of people working relative to the number not working (who have to be supported) is important, since it makes it more and more difficult to support the non-working population. This is already a serious problem in many European countries, such as Italy and Germany, due to the aging of their populations and retirements on the one end of the spectrum and the effect of low birth rates on the labor force at the other end. It will be a coming problem in countries like Japan and, much later, the U.S.

As the labor force shrinks relative to the total population, living standards will be adversely affected, since output will have to be distributed among the total population, not just the working population. It will also have important effects on taxation, as the state takes a larger and larger share of the income of the working population to provide for the non-working population.

4. GROWTH OF RESOURCES

For most countries, most resources grow most of the time. This is particularly true of capital stock, education and technology. It has been basically true of labor force, but this is now changing in some advanced industrialized countries which are undergoing or about to undergo population decline. It is more mixed for land (including discovered natural resources), where some countries are usually showing increasing discovered resources such as oil, while others show decreasing natural resources, due to net depletion.

For all of the resources, or factors of production, a net increase or growth during any year requires that the gross increase be larger than the wearing out process, the depreciation or depletion – the losses during the year.

For all of the resources, or factors of production, growth requires that a portion of the country's output produced be set aside to make possible a net increase in that factor of production,

The process is most easily described for capital stock. The amount of capital stock newly produced during the year – the factories, the machinery and equipment, the commercial buildings, the increase in inventories – is called gross investment. However, the existing stock of capital partially wears out, or becomes obsolescent, during the year. This wearing out process is called depreciation. So, an estimate of the amount of this wearing out process of the capital stock (or, the factor of production, capital) – i.e. depreciation – must be subtracted from gross investment to determine net investment, or the increase in capital stock during the year.

Similarly, growth in the stock of education, which is incorporated in human beings, requires that part of the national output in any year be set aside to provide education. However, this is the gross increase in the stock of education. In order to get the net increase we must make a number of subtractions. First, we have to subtract the stock of education incorporated in those who die. Second, we must subtract an allowance for education which is forgotten during the year. Third, we must subtract an allowance for obsolescence of education. Fourth, we add the stock of education of immigrants and subtract that of emigrants. This gives us the net increase in the stock of education of the population as a whole during the year.

However, what is relevant from the production point of view is the educational stock of the employed labor force. Hence, we have to adjust the foregoing to focus of the employed labor force itself. The gross increase in the stock of education of the employed labor force equals the stock of education incorporated in those who enter the employed labor force during the year plus the increase in the stock of education of those already in the employed labor force. To get the net increase, or growth, in the stock of education of those in the labor force we have to subtract the stock of education of those who leave the employed labor force due to death, retirement, job loss or other reasons. We also have to subtract an allowance for obsolescence of education for labor force members.

For technology, too, growth requires that a part of the national output be set aside to "invest" in technology. The clearest example is expenditure on R & D (research and development). But this is the gross increase in technology. From this must be subtracted an allowance for obsolescence. This is particularly important in technology. No one, for example, produces computers with vacuum tube technology any more.

Just as education is incorporated in human beings, most technology must be incorporated in capital equipment to be used in the process of production. But technological progress tends to be continuous. As a result, when old equipment is replaced by new equipment, newer technology is generally incorporated in the new equipment. So, even if there is no increase in the capital stock, there will be an increase in the stock of technology as worn-out, depreciated equipment is replaced by new equipment which incorporates new technology.

Technology tends to be more internationalized than the other factors of production. This means that countries can benefit from technological progress made elsewhere in the world. There are many ways in which this occurs – e.g. purchase of technologically advanced equipment abroad, importation of new technological knowledge through multinational firms or in other ways, diffusion of scientific knowledge across the world, etc. One of the major home computer producers, for example, is located in Taiwan.

Finally, growth in "land" (natural resources) also requires that a portion of the national output be set aside to find new resources through the process of discovery.

The gross increase, or growth, in "land" (resources) is the increase in discovered resources during a year. To ascertain the net increase, we have to subtract the amount of resources used up during the year, i.e. the depletion of resources. Some countries have substantial net increases due to major discoveries of oil, gold, diamonds and other natural resources. Other countries show decreases as their resources are used up, or depleted, and not offset by new discoveries.

To summarize, growth in the factors of production requires that a portion of national output be set aside to devote to this growth, i.e. to the future. The greater the percentage of the national output set aside, the faster will be growth in the factors of production – land (natural resources), capital, education and technology – and the greater will be growth in these four factors of production relative to labor supply and population.

5. GROWTH OF OUTPUT

Output depends on inputs. Growth of output depends on growth of inputs. So, growth of national output depends on growth in the services of the factors of production, which in turn depends on growth in the actual factors of production.

Most investigators believe that, if all the factors of production grow at the same rate, then output will also grow at the same rate. Of course, this doesn't occur very often in real life.

What happens when one of the factors grows, while the others do not? Under most circumstances, output will still go up, but not in proportion. As the supply of the expanding factor grows relative to the other (static) factors, the additional output produced per additional unit of the expanding factor becomes less and less, eventually reaching zero. If still more of the expanding factor is added, output may actually decline.

This is a famous law of economics, the law of diminishing returns. It was developed in 18th century England when economists considered the addition of more and more laborers to a fixed piece of land. Today, there may be some overpopulated countries where the addition of still more labor to the fixed amount of agricultural land produces no additional output at all. However, in practice this causes migration to the cities where this additional labor usually manages to eke out a precarious living in the service sector, producing at least something, however little and inadequate.

In the industrialized countries, over the past two centuries, the stock of capital has grown faster than the labor supply. This means that each worker has worked with a greater and greater supply of capital over the years, i.e. the capital to labor ratio has increased tremendously.

Economists have reasoned that the law of diminishing returns should apply, as the ratio of the factor of production, capital, to the factor of production, labor, keeps increasing. In other words, they anticipated a lesser and lesser increase in output per increase in the capital stock to labor ratio.

Historically, this hasn't happened. There are two main reasons. First, the stock of technology (which is difficult to measure) has also increased tremendously over the time period. Most technology is incorporated in capital equipment. When there is a net increase in the stock of capital, and even when there is just a replacement of existing capital stock which has worn out, the new capital stock necessarily incorporates additional technology. Personal computers are not replaced by the same old model; they are replaced by new models with advanced features incorporating new technology. The old model has gone out of production.

As a result, historically, it has not been true that the ratio of the same old capital stock to labor increased, triggering the law of diminishing returns. Actually, what has increased is the ratio of capital stock-cum-technology relative to the labor supply. Another way of looking at this is to say that the simultaneous increase in the stock of technology counterbalanced the law of diminishing returns as applied to the ratio of the factor of production, capital, to labor.

The second reason why the law of diminishing returns did not operate, historically, is the growth in the stock of education, which is incorporated in the labor force. A worker today is very different from a worker fifty or a hundred years ago. He is far better educated, far better able to work with advanced technology. So, the tremendous increase in the stock of education, simultaneous with increase in the stock of capital, also offsets application of the law of diminishing returns to the increase in the capital to labor ratio.

The net result of all this appears to be that the ratio of capital stock to output, far from declining, has remained more or less constant in most industrialized countries, over extended periods of time. To be sure, there are fluctuations, but the average does not appear to have changed a lot. This is to say that the growth in the stock of technology and the growth in the stock of education have offset the law of diminishing returns applicable to the increase in the stock of capital relative to the size of the labor force. Net result: the capital/output ratio has remained more or less constant. (Some investigators believe that the capital/output ratio has actually declined in the past two centuries.)

Economists subsume all this into so-called production functions that relate the inputs of the factors of production to output of GDP in mathematical terms. The most popular of these is the Cobb-Douglas production function.

When the growth rate of the factors of production declines, then the growth rate of output also declines. In the US, for example, the decline in the growth rate of the capital stock from the mid-seventies to the mid-nineties is often cited as one of the causal elements of decline in the growth rate of national output during this period (though there are other, more important, reasons). However, it should be realized that the decline in the growth rate of the capital stock also implies at least some decline in the growth rate of the stock of technology, since most technology is incorporated in capital stock.

6. GROWTH IN LIVING STANDARDS

Growth in living standards does not depend on growth of output alone. It depends on growth of output per capita. So, it also depends on how fast the population is growing.

If the growth rate of output is greater than the growth rate of population, living standards can rise. If the growth of output is equal to the growth rate of population, living standards remain constant. If the growth rate of output is less than the growth rate of population, living standards fall.

We already know that the growth rate of national output depends on the growth rate of the factors of production, which in turn depends on the proportion of the national output set aside to provide growth in capital stock, growth in technology, growth in education and growth in discovered natural resources. The greater the proportion of the national product set aside to provide for the future – i.e. to increase the supply of these factors of production – the greater will be the growth in output. Growth rate of output also depends on the growth rate of the labor force, which depends on the demographics of the growth rate of population.

But, if the growth in population is large enough to eat up the entire growth in output, then there will be no increase in output per capita and no increase in living standards.

The term, "economic growth', is usually applied only when there is an increase in output per capita, i.e. when the growth rate in output is greater than the growth rate in population.

It is difficult for those underdeveloped countries which have a high rate of population increase to achieve economic growth. The trouble is that the increase in the labor force and in population has to be equipped with the same capital stock, technology, education, and natural resources as the existing labor force and population to keep per capita income constant. As a result, most of what is set aside of national production to provide for the future, i.e. for increase in the factors of production, is needed to provide the increasse in labor force and in population with the same factors of production as the existing labor force and population. In some cases, the society is simply unable or unwilling to set aside even that much.

As a result, in these countries, economic growth, in terms of growth in output per capita, can be very small, zero, or even negative. In order to speed up economic growth, or achieve economic growth at all, these countries require faster growth in the factors of production – capital stock, technology, stock of education, and discovered natural resources – and/or lower growth in population. Either the one, or the other, or a combination of both will result in an improvement in economic growth and in the standard of living.

The lower the living standards in a country, the more difficult it is in principle to set aside a portion of the national output large enough to result in economic growth and in increase in living standards. Poor countries have intrinsic difficulties in devoting much of their national product to investment in the future, i.e. in increasing the stock of the factors of production, because that leaves even less to consume in the present, with living standards already low.

In effect, a choice must be made between present consumption and future growth in consumption. The less is consumed now, and the larger the share of the national product set aside to increase the factors of production, the greater can be consumption in the future, as a result of the expansion of the national product in future years.

There are many factors that affect the proportion of a country's national product devoted to increasing the factors of production. These include: poverty or wealth of the country; entrepreneurial activity; government taxation policy; extent of the market; public attitudes towards consumption; the work ethic; strength of its legal system; existence of solid property rights; etc. etc.

Lastly, it is easier for countries with low rates of population increase (or even decrease, in some advanced industrialized countries) to expand living standards, since they don't have to equip much of an increase in numbers with the same factors of production already enjoyed by the existing population. They can devote most, or all, of the increase in the factors of production to raising the ratio of these factors to the labor force, producing increased output per capita and increased living standards.

7. ACTUAL AND POTENTIAL OUTPUT

Actual output of the economy is almost always less than capacity output. That is to say that almost every economy could produce more than it is currently producing.

The term, "potential output" is used in two rather different senses. First, we use it in the sense of maximum capacity of the economy to produce. This maximum, or "capacity" output, is achieved only in the middle of a major war when there is maximum pressure on the economy to produce as much as possible. In the U.S., this last happened in 1944.

More frequently used is the term, "full employment" output, i.e. the output of the economy at "full employment". But what is full employment output, often also called the "natural" rate of output, or the NAIRU ("non-accelerating inflation rate of unemployment") rate of output?

In the mid-nineties, full employment in the U.S. was thought to occur when the officially measured rate of unemployment was around 5.5%. But, there were always differences of opinion about this number. Some economists thought that it was somewhat higher, others that it was somewhat lower. Furthermore, the exact number does not remain constant over the passage of time. It depends on the state of the labor market and on economic conditions. More recently, majority opinion has shifted to a somewhat smaller number, around 5% or so.

Full employment (specifically the NAIRU approach) is also said to occur when an unemployment rate is reached such that any further reduction in it would increase, or "accelerate", the rate of inflation.

Finally, full employment (specifically the natural rate approach) is said to be that rate which the economy tends to approach in the long run. (More formally, it is that rate of output where expectations of future inflation equal the actual future inflation subsequently experienced.)

So, to summarize: capacity output is only reached under great wartime pressures; full employment output is often reached; actual output may be less than, equal to or greater than full employment output (but never greater than capacity output). However, if actual output becomes greater than full employment output, there is a tendency for inflation to speed up under most circumstances, unless there are compensating factors, for example, exchange rate appreciation making imports less expensive.

8. THE DETERMINATION OF ACTUAL OUTPUT

What determines the actual output of the economy in any one year? And…will that output be at a level less than full employment, at full employment, or at a level greater than full employment?

To answer these questions we have to look at both supply of and demand for output.

During a period as short as a year, the factors of production – land(and discovered natural resources), labor, capital, education and technology – are more or less fixed. This means that they can produce an output level, or supply of national output, of any quantity up to the capacity level of the economy.

But, the demand for output is not fixed. So, it will be the demand side that determines the amount of national output purchased and produced.

The demand for national output is exercised by different groups – consumers, business, government, and net exports (or net imports).

Consumers are by far the largest group. They purchase roughly two-thirds of the national output of the U.S. The demand for national output exercised by consumers as a group depends very largely on their income. The greater is their income, the greater is their consumption. The less is income, the less is consumption. This is a behavioral matter.

The demand for output by consumers is also somewhat affected by consumer wealth. But the total amount of wealth ordinarily does not change a great deal during a year. Yet, there are times when wealth does change substantially in a relatively limited amount of time due to drastic changes in the valuation of assets, such as stocks and real estate. Japan had both a stock market and a real estate "bubble" in the nineties; the US had a stock market bubble at the end of the nineties. These bubbles all collapsed, changing the amount of wealth greatly. Failing such a bubble, knowledge of the wealth of consumers as a group adds relatively little to explanations of total consumer demand, once we know the effect of consumer incomes on demand.

The demand for output by consumers is also affected by their expectations of future economic conditions. Very occasionally, indeed relatively rarely, consumer expectations change drastically during a year. Insofar as this may happen, it will affect consumer demand.

The second important group is business. Business purchases newly constructed capital goods, such as factories, commercial buildings, machine tools, apartment houses, etc; business also purchases any increase in inventories during the year. All this is called investment. Investment includes all construction activity, including any houses built "to order" by private parties. Gross investment is the gross amount. Net investment equals gross investment minus depreciation. Net investment equals the net increase in the capital stock of the country, i.e. in the factor of production, capital.

Gross investment by business has ranged from about 15% to 18% of gross domestic output in recent years, and net investment about ten percentage points less (due to depreciation).

The demand for investment depends on the behavior of business. Basically, in considering any investment project, business compares the financing cost with the estimated rate of return. If the estimated rate of return exceeds the financing cost (also known as "the cost of capital"), then the project is worthwhile. If not, then the project will not proceed.

So, the demand for investment by business depends on two factors. First, it depends on the interest rate (which is closely related to the financing cost). The higher the interest rate, the higher will be the financing cost and the lower the demand for investment. The lower the interest rate, the lower will be the financing cost and the higher the demand for investment.

Second, the demand for investment depends on the estimated rate of return from investment projects. It must be emphasized that this rate of return is not a fact; it is an estimate which is substantially dependent on the outlook for the future. If business develops – for whatever reason – a very positive outlook, then the estimates of future sales and profits, hence the rate of return, will be high. We then have an "investment boom". If business develops a very negative outlook, then estimates of future sales and profits, hence the rate of return, will be low. We then have an "investment bust". (The biggest "bust" was that which occurred during the Great Depression in the early 1930's.

Since business outlook can vary substantially, so can the demand for investment. As a result, investment is a more fluctuating component of demand than consumption.

A special word needs to be said about one component of investment, namely the change in inventories. There are two reasons why there are changes in inventories. (a) There may be a planned change in inventories, i.e. a business demand for an increase, or a decrease in inventories. (b) There may be, and often are, unplanned changes in inventories. For example, actual sales may be greater than planned sales; the result is an unplanned decline in inventories. Conversely, actual sales may be less than planned sales; the result is an unplanned increase in inventories. As a result, the inventory component of investment – i.e. the increase or decrease in inventories can undergo substantial fluctuations.

The third important group is government. This includes all governmental units – Federal, State and Local Government, as well as special governmental units such as independent government Authorities.

Federal governmental expenditures on goods and services include purchases of weaponry and supplies for the armed services, payment of wages and salaries to armed services personnel, and operation of the civilian sector of the government. State and Local governmental expenditures include provision of primary, secondary and some university education, police and fire protection, etc. Due to the governmental structure in the U.S., the expenditures on goods and services of State and Local Governments are actually considerably greater than those of the Federal Government.

It should be emphasized that governmental expenditures on goods and services in the U.S. account for only about half of all governmental expenditures. The other half are transfer payments, i.e. largely income redistributions of one sort or another, and interest payments on governmental debt.

Total governmental demand for and expenditures on goods and services depend largely on complex political interactions and decisions, such as the size of the armed forces, the size of educational expenditures, the magnitude of a vast variety of governmental programs, etc. They also depend on the willingness to tax the public to pay for those expenditures and the willingness to run governmental deficits, i.e. to borrow in the financial marketplace.

The fourth and last important group involves exports and imports.

The demand for exports derives from foreigners who wish to purchase American goods and services. This demand depends on economic conditions in other countries. It also depends on the types of goods and services which we offer, and on the price of the dollar in terms of the currencies of foreign countries, i.e. on the dollar exchange rates. The more expensive the dollar in terms of foreign currencies, the less will be our exports. Conversely, the cheaper the dollar in terms of foreign currencies, the greater will be our exports.

The demand for imports comes from U.S. residents who wish to purchase foreign goods and services. This demand depends on economic conditions in the U.S. and on our propensity to import, i.e. the degree to which we spend each additional dollar of our income on imports. If U.S. income is higher, our imports are higher. Conversely, if U.S. income is lower, our imports are lower. And, if our propensity to import is higher, our imports are higher. Conversely, if it is lower, our imports are lower. In the last few decades, with the internationalization of trade, the U.S. propensity to import has risen. We now spend a larger share of additional income on imports than was true thirty or forty years ago.

Our demand for imports also depends on the types of goods and services offered by foreign countries, and on the price of foreign currencies in terms of the dollar, i.e. on the dollar exchange rates. The more expensive foreign currencies are in terms of the dollar, the less will be our imports. Conversely, the less expensive foreign currencies are in terms of the dollar, the greater will be our imports.

The net foreign trade balance may be either positive (an export surplus) or negative (an import surplus). The U.S. has had an import surplus for several decades.

An export surplus means that there is a net foreign demand for U.S. goods and services, i.e. foreign demand for U.S. goods and services exceeds U.S. demand for foreign goods and services. An import surplus means that there is a net U.S. demand for foreign goods and services, i.e. U.S. demand for foreign goods and services exceeds foreign demand for U.S. goods and services.

To summarize, there are four different groups which exercise demand for output. These are: consumers, business, government and net exporters (or net importers). Each of these has different behavioral characteristics. National output produced is determined, in any one year, by the addition of consumer demand, investment demand, government demand and net export demand (or minus net import demand). The resulting national output may be less than, equal to, or more than the full employment output level.

There is another way of looking at these matters.

For every act of investment, there must be a counterpart, in an act of saving. Investment means that part of the national output is devoted to increasing the stock of capital. Hence that part is not available for consumption, i.e. that part of national income must be saved.

Savings may be divided into two parts: private savings and government savings (or dissavings). Another name for government savings is the budget surplus of Federal, State and Local Governments. Another name for government dissavings is the government deficit. Since governments everywhere typically run deficits, government dissaving usually is the order of the day. So, national savings equal private savings minus government dissavings. (If there is a government surplus, national savings equal private savings plus the government surplus). We may also say that national savings equal private sector savings minus public sector dissavings (or plus public sector savings). It is national savings which is the counterpart of investment. (Note: investment means private sector investment.)

What happens when we include foreign trade? If the country has an export surplus, i.e. exports of goods and services exceed imports of goods and services, then there has to be a counterpart within domestic national savings to the export surplus, since net exports are not available for domestic consumption.

This means that domestic national savings equal the sum of domestic investment plus the export surplus. In other words, domestic private sector savings minus public sector dissavings (or plus public sector savings) are the counterpart of domestic investment plus the country's export surplus (which is often called the country's "foreign investment", i.e. acquisition of ownership of foreign assets).

If our country has an import surplus, the opposite pertains. An import surplus makes possible domestic investment which exceeds its counterpart of domestic national savings. But, an import surplus means that there is an equal export surplus in some other country. And, that export surplus must have, as its counterpart, domestic savings in that foreign country. So, a nation with an import surplus has as its counterpart foreign savings equal to its import surplus.

This means that domestic investment equals the sum of domestic national savings plus the foreign savings which equal our import surplus. In other words, domestic investment is made possible by domestic private sector savings minus domestic public sector dissavings, plus the foreign savings which equal our import surplus.

Still another way of putting this is to focus on the sum total of domestic investment and government dissavings (i.e. the government deficit). Both of these use up resources which, therefore, are not available for consumption. In other words, they must have, as their counterpart, savings. So, the sum total of domestic investment and the government deficit (government dissavings) must equal domestic private sector savings plus the import surplus (foreign savings equal to it).

To summarize, there are four different groups which save or invest. These are: consumers, government, business and net importers (or exporters). Each of these have different behavioral characteristics. National output is determined by the behavior of these four groups. National output will settle at the level where private sector savings minus public sector dissavings (or plus public sector savings) plus the import surplus (which equals foreign savings) equals domestic investment. Alternately – if there is an export surplus – then national output will settle at the level where private sector savings minus public sector dissavings (or plus public sector savings) equals domestic investment plus "foreign investment" (equal to the export surplus). Respectively, these quantities reflect the behavior of consumers, business, government and net imports (or net exports). The resulting national output may be at less than full employment, at full employment or at more than the full employment level.

Next, we want to answer the following question: what happens to national income if, for example, business increases investment expenditures?

If investment goes up by a dollar, income payments to the factors of production, which produce the additional output, also go up by a dollar. These income payments are received by households who own the factors of production. Households, in turn, have some of the additional dollars taxed away by government. The rest is divided between spending on goods and services (i.e. consumption) and savings.

When households spend on consumption, the economy has to increase its output to provide the additional consumer goods and services. This increase in output in turn means that income payments to the factors of production rise by an equal amount; thus providing further increase in income payments to households. Households then divide the additional receipts between taxes to be paid, consumption and savings. This process continues, providing further, but smaller, increases in national income at each stage. All this is not an instantaneous process; it takes time.

What is the final result of the initial increase in investment? National income increases by a multiple of the initial impetus. In practice, this multiple is not very large, being around 1.4 in the U.S. The ratio of the final increase in national income to the original increase in investment (which could have started, for example, with an increase in exports, etc.) is called the "multiplier".

There are also other results. Consumption will rise with the increase in national income. Household savings will also rise with the increase in household income. The government deficit (or government dissavings) will fall due to increased tax collections. Hence, national savings (i.e. private sector savings minus government dissavings) will rise. And, finally, the import surplus will rise as some of the increased income is spent on imports.

This means that the increase in investment is partially made possible by the increase in domestic private sector savings, partially by the increase in tax collections which make the government deficit (i.e. government dissavings) less than would be the case in the absence of this tax effect, and partially by the increase in the import surplus (corresponding to an increase in foreign savings).

What happens when the government decreases its expenditures on goods and services, thus reducing its deficit (i.e. the dissaving by government)? This is a much recommended policy in many countries. The result is a decrease in national income by a multiple which is around 1.4 in the U.S.

There are other results of the process. Consumption will decline with the decline in household incomes. So will personal savings. Government tax collections also drop due to decline in income. This means that the government budget deficit (i.e. government dissavings) will not decline as much as the initial decrease in government expenditures on goods and services (but it will decline). National savings (i.e. personal savings minus government dissavings) will drop. And, finally, the import surplus will decline due to decline in national income.

This means that the initial reduction in government expenditures on goods and services results in a drop in domestic national savings and a drop in the import surplus (corresponding to a drop in foreign savings), which accompanies a decline in national income. But a decline of a dollar in government expenditures on goods and services results in less than a dollar decline in the government deficit, less than a dollar decline in personal domestic savings, less than a dollar decline in the import surplus, and less than a dollar decline in national savings, all accompanying more than a dollar decline (about $1.4 in the U.S.) in national income. Another way of looking at this is to say that domestic investment will now be financed slightly more by domestic national savings and slightly less by foreign savings.

9. MONEY AND INTEREST RATES

"Money makes the world go round".

But, what is money? Obviously it includes the paper currency and the coins that we carry in our wallets, pockets and purses and that business has in its cash registers. It also includes checkable bank deposits (which can be instantly converted into what is known as legal tender, the paper currency that circulates in our society). The sum total of these, plus a minor addition, is known as the M1 money supply in the U.S.

At one time, none of the components of M1 bore any interest. No interest is paid on paper currency or the coinage. And, no interest was paid on any demand deposits (i.e. checkable deposits). But now, there are some types of checkable deposits which do pay at least a little interest, though well below the market rate.

All money is held by somebody. Practically none is floating in the air or littering the ground. There is a demand for (holding) money and a supply of money (for holding). The combination of demand for money and supply of money determines the price of money, i.e. the interest rate.

There is a cost to holding money, namely the interest foregone. Anyone who holds a hundred dollars in money gives up the interest which could be earned by lending out the hundred dollars.

The interest rate determined by the demand for money and the supply of money is known as the short term interest rate. Its determination is said to occur in the "money market". Actually there is more than one short term interest rate. The best known short term interest rates are: the Federal Funds rate, which refers to overnight borrowing by banks from each other; the Treasury bill rates (e.g. the 3 month Treasury bill rate), which refer to the rates on U.S. Treasury borrowing for one year or less; and the dollar LIBOR (London Interbank Offer Rate), interest rate, which refers to short term interbank borrowing of (Euro)dollars. The "money market" interest rates refer to borrowing which is a year or less in length.

The supply of M1 money in the U.S. is determined by the Federal Reserve (the "Fed"). More specifically, it is determined by the Open Market Committee of the Fed. This consists of 19 members and generally meets every six weeks. The 12 voting members consist of the 7 Governors of the Fed and the President of the Federal Reserve Bank of New York, plus 4 out of the remaining 11 presidents of the 12 Regional Federal Reserve Banks on rotating basis. The Committee sets general policy which is then carried out on a day to day basis by the Federal Reserve Bank of New York.

The basic operating mode of the Open Market Committee, for well over a decade, has been to set a target interest rate and then vary the money supply accordingly to hit that target. In effect, the Fed adjusts the supply of money to hit a specific Federal Funds rate. This target Federal Funds rate is varied from time to time, according to economic conditions.

The demand for M1 money is substantially determined by economic conditions. The principal demand for money is for transactions purposes. We need to carry money with us and have money in our bank accounts for day-to-day, week-to-week, month-to-month transactions that occur all the time. Business needs money in its cash registers and its bank accounts to service customers and pay its bills.

There is a second demand for M1 money, namely for illegal purposes, including both the classical illegal activities and activities which are legal by themselves, but involve tax evasion. This latter demand particularly involves the currency portion of M1. Included are both demand for M1 for illegal transactions and for temporary storage of tax-evasion wealth. This whole subject is usually discussed under the heading of the subterranean, underground, or black economy.

There is also a third demand for M1 money (for the currency component), transactions and storage of wealth in some foreign countries. This foreign demand for U.S. currency means that part of the U.S. money supply is not available to meet domestic demand for money.

In former days, economists also added two other demands for money, a speculative demand for money and a precautionary demand for money. The basic idea of the former was that speculators would keep on hand a supply of M1 money to take advantage of any opportunities that might arise. And, as a precaution, just about anyone might keep on hand a supply of M1 money in case of any unforeseen contingencies that required money. But today, these two groups keep on hand interest bearing assets such as money market funds or Treasury bills which can be converted almost instantly into money. Hardly anyone keeps on hand hoards of money any more for such purposes.

The demand for money and the supply of money jointly determine the (short term) interest rate. What happens to the interest rate as economic conditions change? As the economy enters an upswing and national income rises, the demand for money also rises and, with it, the interest rate. Usually, the Fed partially "accomodates", i.e. increases the growth rate of the money supply somewhat, but not enough to eliminate the rise in interest rates. Conversely, as the economy enters recession, the demand for money drops and so does the interest rate.

There are short term, medium term and long term interest rates. A short term interest rate is one which pertains to a loan contract a year or less in length. A medium term interest rate usually is considered to be one which pertains to a loan contract one to ten years in length. A long term interest rate is one which pertains to a loan contract in excess of ten years.

Short, medium and long term interest rates are related. Usually, the long term interest rates are highest, the medium term interest rates next and the short term interest rates lowest. This is the "normal" situation. Long term government bonds have the greatest risk for the holder, since they fluctuate more in market price; hence they bear the highest interest rates to reward the holder for bearing the highest risk. The medium term financial instruments (or government "notes") are intermediate in market price fluctuation, risk and interest rates; and the short term government "bills" fluctuate very little in price; hence they have the lowest risk and the lowest interest rates.

However, there are economic circumstances when short, medium and long term interest rates are much the same, and occasionally even times when short term interest rates exceed medium and long term interest rates.

Usually, when short term interest rates go up, long term interest rates also go up, but by a lesser percentage; there is no one-to-one correspondence between the rise in short and long term interest rates. In fact, sometimes these rates may move in opposite directions. The same pertains to a downward swing in interest rates.

The long term interest rate is closely related to the cost of financing investment projects, such as new plants, commercial buildings, and production equipment. Since most investment projects last for a considerable period of time, they usually require long term financing. So, when long term interest rates go up, the cost of financing investment projects also goes up; this – by itself – has negative impact on investment projects.

Most short and intermediate term interest rates are more closely related to the cost of financing consumer purchases, for example automobiles. Credit card debt also comes under this category.

When the Fed wants to cool down the economy it decreases the growth rate of the supply of money and, hence, increases short term interest rates, through what are known as open market operations. These involve decreasing the ability of the banks to create checkable deposits, thus the money supply.

When the economy is in an expansionary phase, the demand for money rises, since transactions rise. This causes an increase in short term interest rates. As noted earlier, usually the Fed partially accomodates the increased demand by increasing the growth rate of the money supply somewhat; the short term interest rate rises, but not as fast as it would in the absence of this partial accomodation by the Fed. The long term interest rate usually also rises.

What happens to investment? The cost of financing is up. But, investment depends on the relationship between the expected future return and the cost of financing. Due to the expansion of the economy, business expectations of future profits will rise and so will the expected rate of return. As a result, investment usually will be up, despite the increase in the cost of financing. And, indeed, the rise in investment becomes an important factor in the economic upswing.

At this point, we must make a distinction between real interest rates and nominal interest rates. Basically, the real interest rate equals the nominal interest rate minus the expected rate of inflation. The nominal interest rates can be looked up in the newspaper. The real interest rates have to be calculated, To take an example, an expected rate of inflation of 3 per cent results in a nominal interest rate which is 3 per cent greater than the real interest rate.

As noted earlier, the Fed has been targeting the Federal Funds rate. This is a short term nominal interest rate. If the Fed targets the Federal Funds rate at 5.5 per cent, and the expected short term rate of inflation is 3 per cent, then the Fed is effectively targeting at a 2.5 per cent real short term interest rate.

It has previously been noted that interest rates tend to rise in a business upswing. This refers to both real and nominal rates. Demand for money rises relative to supply of money, increasing real interest rates. In addition, during a business upswing expectations of inflation will rise eventually, increasing nominal interest rates further.

But, under unusual conditions, inflationary expectations may actually fall, resulting in declining nominal interest rates in the face of rising real interest rates. This was the U.S. position around 1997/8.

10. INFLATION

Inflation exists when there is a continuing rise in prices. Inflations may be very small – a few per cent annually – or very large – thousands of per cent annually or even more.

In industrialized countries, inflations are generally very modest. But, they are ubiquitous. Since the end of the Second World War, prices have risen in nearly every industrialized country nearly every year. In the underdeveloped countries, in contrast, inflations are far more likely to be more severe, very occasionally even reaching wild extremes called hyperinflations. Under highly unusual and rare conditions, e.g. the sequel of a major war, even industrialized countries may experience wild inflation. Fortunately, the vast majority of all inflations are very small, or somewhat larger, but still manageable.

Inflations are generally accompanied by increases in the money supply. But there is no simple one-to-one correspondence between increase in money supply and inflation. For very small inflations – growth rates of prices of a few per cent annually – inflation is usually less than the growth rate of the money supply relative to the growth rate in real (i.e. deflated) national product. But, for larger and larger inflations, it is more and more likely that inflations are actually greater than the growth rate of the money supply relative to the growth rate of the real national product.

In some sense, high inflations are "caused" by increase in the money supply. But, behind this factor are deeper causal elements, usually government deficits financed by printing money or equivalent methods of finance. This is particularly true where wild inflations occur.

Small inflations tend to become "built-in". For example, if the "built-in" inflation in an economy is 3 per cent, the actual inflation rates over a period of years are likely to be within a percentage point or two downwards and a few percentage points upwards of this figure. Basically the cost structure of the economy moves upwards more or less by the "built-in" inflation rate each year. In particular, union wage negotiations and non-union personnel reviews wind up with a wage or salary increase (above the growth rate in national productivity) approximately of the "built-in" percentage. And…after a few years, public anticipations of expected inflation also settle roughly at the "built-in" percentage rate of inflation.

Inflations come in two varieties – expected and unexpected. In an expected inflation, all the prices, in principle, move up in tandem, except, of course, money itself. As a result, there is no redistribution of income or wealth, except for the holders of currency and non-interest bearing bank accounts who lose out. In practice, no inflation is precisely a hundred per cent anticipated. So, there are always some redistribution effects.

In an inflation which is unanticipated in whole or in part, there can be very substantial redistribution effects for both income and assets. In such an inflation, debtors gain and creditors lose, unless the debts are fully adjusted, or indexed, for inflation. Basically, the debtors get to repay the creditors in less valuable money. So, assets which involve a fixed price – such as bonds which are redeemed at a stated amount, or money itself, go down in real value. In contrast, assets which are likely to adjust to inflation – such as real estate, stocks or inflation indexed debt – generally maintain their value (but stocks in particular can go down in real value for substantial periods of time before recovering). Those who own assets, e.g. housing, which maintain their real value, and carry debts on those assets, which go down in real value (e.g. fixed interest rate mortgages), can benefit greatly from inflation.

Another popular way of looking at inflation is to contrast demand inflation with supply inflation. Demand inflation occurs when demand exceeds supply at the existing price level, for example the demand inflation of the latter 1960's when the U.S. tried to produce both "guns" and "butter" (the Vietnamese War and the Great Society) at the same time. Supply inflation occurs when production costs, such as materials or labor costs, keep on rising. Good examples are the oil price induced cost increases of the 1970's. In practice, demand inflation and cost inflation tend to interact, producing the so-called inflationary spiral. Once started, it quite often becomes all but impossible to disentangle demand induced from cost induced price rises. It is the chicken and egg problem.

Inflation also distorts the tax system, unless the system is fully indexed for inflation. For example, inflation throws taxpayers into higher income tax brackets and, hence, increases real taxes on individuals without any changes in their real incomes.

Inflation affects nominal interest rates. Nominal interest rates are those which are used in the financial world and are quoted daily in the newspapers. A nominal interest rate equals the real interest rate plus the expected rate of inflation. This means that nominal interest rates exceed the rate of inflation. The real interest rate is the inflation adjusted interest rate, which has to be estimated from data. In practice, nominal interest rates can fluctuate far more than real interest rates. (This is true for all but very large inflations.) Since tax systems generally focus on nominal interest rates, inflation can greatly distort the tax system.

What does the inflationary process look like for industrialized countries with relatively modest rates of inflation?

First of all, we have to consider the relationship of inflation to real (inflation adjusted) national output. As national output increases and becomes closer to "full employment", there will be a slow increase in pressure on use of resources which may affect inflation very slightly. Typically, inflation will remain just about at its "built-in" amount. Then, after the economy reaches "full employment" and moves beyond it, pressure on resources increases. For example, employers may have to entice workers away from other employers at higher wages. As a result, the rate of inflation picks up somewhat. If the economy increases still more, inflation will as well.

But what is the full employment rate of output (also called the "natural" rate of output)? Basically, if the economy expands further, above this output level, inflation will "accelerate". Hence, another name for the full employment output level is the NAIRU ("non-accelerating inflation rate of unemployment) level of output.

What can be said about the actual numbers implied by the concept of full employment? What is the unemployment rate that corresponds to the concept of full employment (or NAIRU)?

First, the actual magnitude of this unemployment rate can differ greatly in different countries. In the 1990's it has been far greater in most Western European countries than in the U.S. Second, it varies somewhat over time, depending on the state of the labor market, the state of the materials markets, the structure of the economy, the degree of corporate restructuring and other factors. Third, there is always some difference of opinion on the exact number of this unemployment rate. For example, a common number in the early 1990's was 6 per cent for the U.S., with a range of views around it. A few years later, more and more economists revised this downwards, to perhaps 5.5 per cent. Still later, economists increasingly began to think that it might then be as low as 5.0 per cent.

What happens when output rises beyond the unemployment rate corresponding to full employment? We have already stated that inflation will tend to speed up as pressure on scarce resources rises. Hence, the actual experienced inflation will be greater than the anticipated inflation rate.

As a result, when the next round of union wage bargaining occurs and the next series of non-union wage and salary reviews take place, higher wage and salary increases result as labor makes up the difference between the actual and the anticipated inflation rates. These wage increases are then reflected in price increases. So, inflation takes a jump. The process continues as long as national output is beyond the full employment point. It leads to higher and higher inflation (the inflationary spiral). The process reverses once national output dips below the full employment level, and the inflationary spiral comes down, eventually reaching the "built-in" rate of inflation, or even somewhat less. But, at the end of this process the actual price level will be considerably higher than it was at the beginning.

To summarize: with a "built-in" rate of inflation, the price level itself moves steadily upwards. If there is, in addition, an inflationary spiral, the price level can increase far more. This happened in the U.S. in the 'seventies and early 'eighties.

One further word needs to be said about the level of "built-in" inflation. First, it is obviously affected by the way in which the government measures inflation. In the 'nineties, the U.S. government revised the calculation of the consumer price index, in effect lowering it by more than half a percentage point. This alone changed the 3 per cent to slightly less than 2.5 per cent. Second, "built-in" inflation is affected by extraneous factors, for example, the foreign exchange rate. A rising dollar makes imports cheaper, which is a factor tending to reduce inflation. This will lower the "built-in" inflation, as long as the dollar keeps rising in value. There will be a reversal when the dollar starts falling.

11. GOVERNMENT

Government is always extremely important for the economy. Government sets the rules of the game. Without adequate rules and enforcement, the economy cannot thrive.

Government provides the stage on which the economy operates. Property rights, a system of commercial law, impartial courts to settle disputes, physical safety through adequate law enforcement, reasonable regulations by competent bureaucrats, minimal bribery, transparency, all these and more are required for a healthy economy. Where these are less than adequate, for example physical safety in Russia, strong negatives may result.

Governments practically everywhere make two types of expenditures: purchases of goods and services; and transfer payments.

Purchases of goods and services by government include both capital goods type expenditures such as government buildings, planes for the military and naval vessels, and consumption type expenditures such as police and fire protection, educational expenditures, salaries of military personnel and the operational costs of the White House.

Transfer payments to households and business such as Social Security, farm subsidies and welfare expenditures, are payments which do not require any immediate service by the recipient in return for the payment. The salary of a high school teacher is a purchase of a service by government. In contrast, the payment of unemployment compensation is a government transfer payment. Transfer payments have been the fastest growing government expenditures in practically all industrialized countries. (Interest on the national debt is a special kind of transfer payment.)

These government expenditures on goods and services and on transfer payments have to be financed. Typically, most government expenditures are financed by taxes in the industrialized countries. These include income taxes, sales taxes, value added taxes, social security taxes, medicare taxes, property taxes, excise taxes (on gasoline, cigarettes, liquor, etc.), tariffs and still more. The proportion of national income appropriated by government through the tax system has grown tremendously in the last seventy years almost everywhere in the world. So, governments use a much higher proportion of the national product today than was true in the past.

It turns out that tax collections are usually not sufficient to finance all of government expenditures. The rest is financed by borrowing and by printing money or its financial equivalent.

This shortfall of government tax revenues relative to government expenditures is called the government deficit. Nearly all governments have deficits nearly all the time. For the developed countries, these deficits are financed through borrowing, with relatively little financed through printing of money. In contrast, for the underdeveloped world, printing money is significantly more important.

Government expenditure on goods and services is one of the four elements of aggregate demand which, together, determine the size of national income and expenditure. (The others are consumption demand, investment demand, and net export demand – or minus net import demand.) But government also affects some of these others directly.

Taxes reduce the income which households have available for spending and saving. So, after taxes, household consumption demand will be less than it would have been in the absence of taxes. Household savings will also be less on an after-tax basis.

In addition, taxes reduce imports, again because they reduce the income available for spending, which, in turn, reduces not only domestic spending but also spending on imports.

More indirectly, taxes may also affect investment demand. When the public has less income available for spending, i.e. less disposable income, business will sell less, hence build fewer and/or smaller factories, houses, equipment, etc.

We have previously detailed (chapter 8) how an increase in investment will increase national income by a multiple. Similarly, an increase in government expenditure on goods and services will increase national income by a multiple. But... income taxes reduce the degree of expansion considerably. This is due to the taxes taken out of the increases in household income.

Government may try to change national output, as well as the unemployment rate, through changes in government expenditures on goods and services, government transfer payments, and tax policy. This is called fiscal policy. Basically, the results are these: an increase in government expenditures on goods and services (which increases demand for national output) will result in an increase in the government deficit, an increase in national income and an increase in consumption; it will also increase private sector savings, due to the increase in national income. Conversely, a decrease in government expenditures on goods and services (which decreased demand for national output) will decrease the government deficit, decrease national income, and decrease consumption; it will also decrease private sector savings, due to the decrease in national income.

An increase in government transfer payments to households will increase the government deficit, increase household demand, hence consumption, and increase national income; it will also increase private sector savings due to the increase in national income. Conversely, a decrease in government transfer payments to households will decrease the government deficit, decrease household demand, hence consumption, and decrease national income; it will also decrease private sector savings due to the decrease in national income.

A decrease in income tax rates will increase the government deficit, increase after-tax household income, hence consumption, and increase national income; it will also increase private sector savings due to the increase in income. In addition, it will increase the multiplier. Conversely, an increase in income tax rates will decrease the government deficit, decrease after-tax household income and decrease national income; it will also decrease private sector savings due to the decrease in income. In addition, it will decrease the multiplier.

All of these results are short run results, i.e. within one business cycle.

But, there is something else that is affected by government fiscal policy, namely inflation. Typically, industrialized economies have a certain, small amount of inflation "built-in" - a few percentage points. If government fiscal policy drives the economy to very high real output levels with very low unemployment rates, the degree of inflation tends to increase. Beyond the "full employment" point, inflation is said to "accelerate".

So, fiscal policy must be careful. If it is too restrictive, the unemployment rate may be unacceptably high. If it is too expansionary, inflation may be unacceptably high.

But…it should be noted that governments often change expenditures and even taxes for reasons which have nothing to do with a conscious fiscal policy. There are many political reasons why governments act in this manner. So, a government may have no fiscal policy worth noting, but there will still be fiscal effects, even without any conscious fiscal policy. Some of these effects can be quite deleterious and counterproductive.

We also want to say a few words about the concept of "national savings", which equal private sector savings minus public sector dissavings (the government deficit). For example, if the government increases its expenditures on goods and services or on transfer payments, the result will be a larger government deficit (larger public sector dissavings), a rise in national income and a rise in private sector savings (which is less than the rise in the government deficit). Hence, there will be a decline in "national savings". Similarly, a tax decrease will result in a rise in public sector dissavings (the government deficit), a rise in national income and a rise in private sector saving (which is less than the rise in the government deficit). Hence there will be a decline in "national savings". All these are short term effects.

Governments affect their economies in many other ways. For example, most Western European Governments make it very expensive for employers to hire labor due to the very heavy taxes the employers must pay for a huge panoply of social benefits. They also have made it both expensive and difficult to fire a worker. As a result, employers would rather not hire in the first place. And, until the latter 'nineties, these governments made it very difficult to hire temporary employees. At the same time, these governments give long term, expensive unemployment and social benefits to those who have lost a job or never found one. The result is a far higher unemployment rate in most Western European countries than in the U.S.

12. DEFICITS AND DEBT

Government deficits must be financed. They may be financed either by borrowing from the financial marketplace (i.e. debt finance), or by printing money or its financial equivalent (i.e. money finance).

The industrialized countries finance almost completely by issuing debt. There is only a modest amount of money finance and this small amount is under the effective control of the central bank which provides for the money needs of the country. However, there have been some historical exceptions, notably the money financed German Government deficits which led to hyperinflation in 1923.

The developing world is far more prone to money finance with its accompanying inflation. Many of these countries have substantial government deficits with little ability to cover these deficits through borrowing.

The size of the government debt in any country has to be compared to the size of the national output. This is done with use of the debt ratio, usually taken as the government debt divided by the gross domestic product (GDP).

There is a difference between net debt and gross debt. Gross debt is the total amount of government debt outstanding. Net debt subtracts that part of the government debt which is held by the government itself or by one of its agencies. In the U.S., the Social Security Trust Funds and the Federal Reserve System as well as other Government trust funds hold large amounts of government debt. All this must be subtracted from the gross figure to get the net amount

In the U.S., the debt ratio was in excess of 100 per cent at the end of the Second World War, declined to about 25 per cent in the mid-seventies, and was somewhat over 50 per cent (net basis) by the mid 'nineties. Subsequently the ratio declined and then started rising again after 9/11. The great decline in the debt ratio from 1945 to 1975 was due to lesser growth rate in the nominal debt than in the nominal GDP. That, in turn, occurred because the government deficits during this period were relatively "small". In contrast, the subsequent rise in the debt ratio after 1975 to the mid-nineties occurred because the government deficits during much of this latter period were relatively "large".

So, for a "small" government deficit, the growth rate of the nominal debt will be less than the growth rate of the nominal GDP; hence the debt ratio declines. For a "large" government deficit, the growth rate of the debt will be greater than the growth rate of the nominal GDP; hence the debt ratio rises. For example, if the debt ratio is 50 per cent and the government deficit is 2% of GDP, then the debt itself will grow at 4% per year. If the real GDP grows at 2.5% per year and inflation is 3%, then nominal GDP grows at 5.5% per year. As a result of faster nominal growth rate in GDP than debt, the debt ratio will decline.

But, if the government deficit is 3% of GDP, with the debt ratio at 50%, then nominal debt itself will grow at 6% annually. With the same growth rates of real GDP and inflation as above, the debt ratio will increase.

What happens when the debt ratio increases to high levels (beyond 100%)? First, holders of government securities will demand higher interest rates, as the risk of holding these securities rises. Then, if the debt ratio goes still higher, foreigners will stop buying the government's securities. It will become more and more difficult to issue dollar denominated debt. Finally, with still higher debt ratios, local-currency denominated debt will be increasingly difficult to sell, as the country's own citizens stop buying government securities. As this process continues, and the government is shut out of both the external (dollar denominated) money market and the internal (mostly local currency denominated) money market, it will have to resort to printing money to finance its deficit.

Does government borrowing have to be repaid at some future time? And is it, in fact, repaid? Generally, the answer is, "no". (The debt will be rolled over, i.e. refinanced.) Borrowing by the government will simply raise the debt ratio, or cause it to decline more slowly.

This is true until the government reaches a maximum ratio of debt to GDP. Any debt beyond that ratio will not be bought by the financial markets. This limits the debt financed government deficit at that point to the amount which results in a growth rate of debt no greater than the nominal growth rate of GDP. However, governments can resort to printing money.

How can a country reduce the debt ratio? First, it can increase taxes and/or cut expenditures, thus lowering the government deficit. Second – for internal debt, denominated in the home currency – it can inflate its way out of at least some of the internal debt, by creating unexpected inflation (hence, increasing nominal national income) which reduces the debt/GDP ratio. Third, it can increase the real growth rate of GDP. Fourth, it can renege on the debt, by simply not paying it in part or in whole. Fifth, it can sell off government property, such as nationalized industries, and use the proceeds to retire debt. None of this is easy. Some of it is very undesirable.

What can be said about deficits and debt for a nation, as compared to households and corporations? Households often run a "deficit", i.e. a year when expenditures exceed income. This is true, for example, when a house or apartment is purchased, since the cost far exceeds income; most of the purchase price has to be financed through borrowing or using past asset accumulations. Corporations often run a "deficit", when their capital expenditures exceed their internal cash flows.

One difficulty is that governments, households and corporations usually use different accounting systems. The Government accounting systems often lump together current expenditures for goods and services (such as pay for armed services personnel), current transfer payments (such as Social Security), and expenditures on capital goods (such as construction of new government buildings). Historically, this was true for the US for decades, but is no longer the case.

A "balanced government budget" requirement means that current expenditures of government plus capital expenditures of government together must equal or exceed government income from taxation. For households, a "balanced budget" under the same definition would make it all but impossible to buy houses or apartments. For corporations, a "balanced budget" requirement would severely restrict capital expenditures; they could be no greater than internally generated cash flow. Neither households nor corporations would be able to borrow much in the financial marketplace under a "balanced budget" restriction, or even use funds accumulated in the past.

13. INTERNATIONAL

Commercial and financial relations between different countries, each with its own currency, involve exchange rates. The exchange rate between two countries shows the value of one currency in terms of the other. It may be given in either direction, for example, 110 Japanese yen per dollar, or 0.0090909 dollars per yen.

Exchange rates may be either fixed or flexible. Fixed exchange rates require day to day intervention by central banks to keep the exchange rate fixed. Flexible exchange rates do not require central bank intervention, but mostly central banks intervene anyway.

For the industrialized countries, exchange rates have basically been flexible (or, floating) since early 1973, and, to some extent, 1971. In the developing world, most countries use fixed exchange rates, which are fixed relative to some other currency (such as the dollar) or basket of currencies.

But, the exchange rates of members of the European Monetary System were nearly fixed relative to each other until the system almost broke down in the early 1990's. Then, it became a flexible exchange rate system, but with fixed limits of fluctuations. From this status, it evolved into a single system (the Eurocurrency) for 12 of its members.

In a flexible exchange rate system, the exchange rate between two countries is determined by demand and supply. This exchange rate determination may be stated in terms of the domestic currency or in terms of the foreign currency. For example, the dollar/yen exchange rate is determined by the demand for U.S. dollars and the supply of U.S. dollars, or, conversely, by the supply of Japanese yen and the demand for Japanese yen.

There are two types of international transactions that affect the demand and supply of currencies – those that derive from trade in goods and services, and those that derive from purchase and sale of financial assets.

On the side of trade in goods and services, any imports into the U.S. require a payment for these imports in terms of foreign currency. So, there is a demand for Japanese yen (which means a supply of dollars to pay for these yen). Any exports from the U.S. to foreign countries require payment by foreigners for these exports. So, there is a demand for U.S. dollars (which means a supply of Japanese yen to pay for the dollars).

Trade in goods and services between countries follows two fundamental rules. First, is the rule of comparative advantage. Countries will export those goods and services in which they have a comparative advantage in production and import those in which some other country has a comparative advantage. So, even if a country has an absolute advantage in several goods, it will only export those in which it has comparative advantage and import those goods whose comparative advantage lies abroad. This leads to international specialization. For example, the U.S. exports wheat and imports bananas.

Second, is the rule of product differentiation combined with economies of scale, Most trade of industrialized countries is with other industrialized countries, much of it in the same industrial classification categories. So we find, for example, autos exported from Italy to Germany and autos exported from Germany to Italy. These autos are not identical; they are different, i.e. differentiated products. Since autos have to be produced in fairly massive quantities to be economic, it is not practical to put an auto manufacturing plant in every country for every auto model. Hence, Fiat produces in Italy, and Volkswagen in Germany.

On the side of purchase and sale of financial assets, any purchase of a foreign asset by U.S. residents (such as a purchase of stock in a foreign company on a foreign stock exchange) requires a payment for these assets in terms of foreign currency. So, there is a demand for Japanese yen (which means a supply of dollars to pay for these yen). Conversely, any purchase of U.S. assets by foreigners requires a payment by foreigners for these assets. So, there is a demand for U.S. dollars (which means a supply of Japanese yen to pay for these dollars).

A purchase by the U.S. of foreign assets is called a U.S. capital export. (It is, of course, a capital import for the other country.) A purchase of U.S. financial assets by foreigners is called a U.S. capital import. (It is a capital export for the other country.)

Such financial transactions (capital imports and capital exports) are essentially divided into two types – those on private account and those due to central banks' intervention in the currency markets.

Private capital flows include all purchases and sales of assets by the private sector. Central bank intervention in dollars (hence, capital flow) includes any purchase and sale of a foreign currency for dollars by foreign central banks or by the U.S. central bank (the Fed).

To summarize, the exchange rate between two currencies is determined by three factors: (a) imports and exports of goods and services; (b) private capital exports and private capital imports; (c) central bank intervention.

At the end of each year, an accounting is published for a country which shows the results of these international transactions. This is called the balance of payments. It also has three parts: (a) the current account; this shows the amount of imports and exports of goods and services (and a small amount of gift items); (b) private sector capital imports and exports (the financial flows) (which also include a small amount of government capital flow transactions); (c) central bank intervention capital flows for both foreign central banks and the Fed.

The three accounts follow a very simple principle for any country. They must add up to zero. So, for example, a deficit on current account (imports exceeding exports) has to be counterbalanced by a surplus on the sum of the private capital account and the central bank intervention account.

Why do central banks intervene? They do so because they want to influence the exchange rate, since the exchange rate is a very important price in the floating exchange rate system used by the major countries. There are many important pressures on central banks to intervene in one direction or the other. Export industries, for example, want the exchange rate to be low, so that foreign customers find the products cheaper (in the foreigners' currencies), hence willing to buy more. On the other hand, industries that compete with imports want the exchange rate to be high, so that imports become more expensive in terms of the domestic currency, hence less competitive.

What determines private capital flows – the purchase and sale of foreign assets by domestic residents, and the purchase and sale of domestic assets by foreign residents?

Here we have to look at some of the big asset markets – the stock market, the bond market, the real estate market, the market for corporate acquisitions and establishment of subsidiaries abroad. This involves expectations.

When the U.S. stock markets are expected to rise (faster than their own), foreigners will tend to sell their own currencies in order to buy dollars which in turn are used to purchase stocks. This tends to increase the dollar exchange rate, i.e. make the dollar more expensive. This is a U.S. capital import. Conversely, when the U.S. stock markets are expected to fall, foreigners will tend to sell U.S. stocks and sell the dollars received in order to purchase their own currencies. This tends to decrease the dollar exchange rate, i.e. make the dollar cheaper. This is a U.S. capital export. Americans will act somewhat similarly, following their own expectations.

When the U.S. real estate markets are expected to rise, foreigners will also tend to sell their currencies and buy dollars which are used to buy U.S. real estate. This again tends to increase the dollar exchange rate, i.e. make the dollar more expensive. This is a U.S. capital import. Conversely, when the U.S. real estate markets are expected to fall, the reverse will occur. There will be capital exports and the dollar exchange rate tends to decrease. i. e. make the dollar cheaper.

Now we come to the bond markets. A bond is a longer term financial debt. Hence this involves longer term interest rates. Longer term interest rates are inversely related to the price of bonds. When longer term interest rates go down, the price of bonds goes up, When longer term interest rates go up, the price of bonds goes down.

Thus, when longer term U.S. interest rates are expected to fall, the price of bonds is obviously expected to rise. When foreigners hold these expectations, they will tend to sell their currencies to buy dollars in order to buy U.S. bonds. This tends to increase the dollar exchange rate, i.e. make the dollar more expensive. This is a U.S. capital import. It is important to realize that an expected fall in long term interest rates will cause the dollar exchange rate to rise, i.e. move in the opposite direction.

Conversely, when longer term U.S. interest rates are expected to rise (hence the price of U.S. bonds expected to fall), foreigners will tend to sell U.S. bonds, sell dollars and buy their own currencies. This is a U.S. capital export. The dollar exchange rate will tend to decrease, i.e. make the dollar cheaper.

When foreign companies want to buy corporations in the U.S. or build U.S. subsidiaries, they will tend to buy dollars so that they can pay for these assets. This is a U.S. capital import. It tends to increase the dollar exchange rate, i.e. make the dollar more expensive. Conversely, when U.S. corporations want to buy foreign corporations or establish subsidiaries abroad, they will sell dollars and buy foreign currencies. This is a U.S. capital export. It tends to decrease the dollar exchange rate, i.e. make the dollar cheaper.

Finally, we want to consider what happens when there are short term interest differentials between countries. (Casual observation shows that this is common in the current flexible exchange rate system, for example between Japan and the U.S.) This brings us to a new concept, the spot exchange rate vs. the forward exchange rate between two countries. The spot exchange rate is the price of one currency in terms of another currency right now. The forward exchange rate is the price of one currency in terms of another currency for delivery of the currency in 90 days, 180 days, or some other point of time in the future. For example, a U.S. importer of French wine who has to pay for his imports in Euros in 90 days can go to his bank and acquire a contract in which the bank promises to deliver the requisite amount in Euros in 90 days. This is called buying forward cover. It protects the U.S. importer against adverse fluctuations in the dollar/Euro exchange rate. The completed transaction is called a covered transaction.

Now we come to the following question: if there is a differential in short term interest rates between two countries, is there any incentive for a flow of capital from the country with the lower interest rate to the country with the higher interest rate?

Here it is best to use an example. A financier in Tokyo (where short term interest rates are lower) can buy spot dollars at the spot dollar/yen exchange rate, lend out these dollars in the U.S. short term money market, say for a year, then bring back the funds to Japan. However, he does not know the future dollar/yen exchange rate that will pertain at the end of the year. To protect himself, against adverse fluctuation in the exchange rate he would need to buy one year forward yen. But, it can be shown that the forward yen will sell at a forward premium over the spot exchange rate that will exactly equal the interest rate differential between the two countries. Whatever is gained on the interest rate differential is lost on the difference between the forward rate and the spot rate. So, there is no incentive to conduct this transaction in the first place.

If the Japanese financier decides to undertake this transaction without buying forward cover, then he obviously is taking his chances on the future dollar/yen exchange rate. Still, as long as the expected future dollar/yen spot exchange rate in a year's time (since the actual future spot exchange rate cannot be known with certainty now) is equal to the current forward rate (which is known now) – which is true most of the time – he will neither gain nor lose on average. But he is taking a risk for which there is no average reward. Hence, there is no incentive for capital flow.

Only under highly unusual conditions will substantial financial flows occur due to short term interest differentials between two countries. (One possibility involves large interest differentials combined with substantially held expectations that the future spot exchange rate will not substantially differ from the current spot rate – a most unlikely combination.)

Which factors - international trade flows in goods and services or financial flows, i.e. capital imports and exports – are the most important in determining the exchange rate in the short run and in the long run?

In the short run, the most important factors are capital flows – the purchase and sale of foreign currencies in order to buy and sell foreign assets. This includes the private capital account, where the private sector buys and sells foreign currencies, and it includes the central bank intervention account, where central banks buy and sell foreign currencies. In today's world, the foreign exchange market is the largest market in the world, well in excess of a trillion dollars a day. As such, it largely tends to determine short term exchange rates.

In the long run, international trade flows in goods and services tend to determine exchange rates. Over the decades, these trade flows impact most heavily on exchange rates. In the long run, some currencies tend to go up and others tend to go down. Over the past half century, the long run trends of the old German D-mark and the Japanese yen were up while the long run trend of the old Italian lira was down. Such long run trends, in turn, are determined by relative degrees of inflation and relative degrees of productivity change in different countries. However, these long run trends have been interrupted by shorter term trends in the opposite direction that sometimes lasted for several years.

There are several different types of exchange rates. Those published in the newspapers are called bilateral nominal exchange rates, for example the dollar/Euro and the dollar/yen exchange rates. But, it may be useful to find what happens to the average exchange rate for a country with most of its important trading partner over a period of time. This average exchange rate is called a multilateral exchange rate, For example, to find the multilateral exchange rate for the U.S., the exchange rate for each important U.S. trading partner is weighted by the sum of U.S. exports to and imports from that country. Then the average is taken for all such countries. This can then be used to find how the average exchange rate has varied over time.

There is also the real bilateral exchange rate between two countries. This is found by adjusting the nominal bilateral exchange rate for the relative degrees of inflation in each of the two countries. The bilateral real exchange rate is necessary to get a more realistic view of the import of changes in the exchange rate. For example, if one country has no inflation and another country has one hundred per cent inflation annually while the value of its currency drops in half, the real bilateral exchange rate remains constant.

Finally, there is the real multilateral exchange rate for a country. This is the average of the real exchange rates with that country's main trading partners. When changes are considered in a country's exchange rate over a period of time, it is the real multilateral exchange rate that must be used.

Exports and imports are both affected by the real multilateral exchange rate. Exports depend on this exchange rate and on business conditions abroad. If the currency of a country is expensive for foreigners, foreigners will buy less and exports will be less. If the currency of a country is cheap for foreigners, foreigners will buy more and exports will be more.

Imports depend on the multilateral exchange rate and on business conditions at home. If the currency of the country is expensive for foreigners then the foreign currency will be cheap for natives; hence, natives will buy more foreign currency to buy more foreign goods; imports will be greater. If the currency of the country is cheap for foreigners then the foreign currency will be expensive for natives; hence, natives will buy less foreign currency and less foreign goods; imports will be less.

Imports also depend on domestic business conditions. If the economy is doing very well and the country is at full employment, consumers in the country will buy more imports. If the economy is in recession and incomes are less, then consumers will buy less imports. When national income goes up, imports also go up.

A country may have an export surplus (exports greater than imports) or an import surplus (imports greater than exports). An export surplus is almost the same as a current account surplus. (A small adjustment needs to be made for gifts; these are included in the current account but not in exports or imports.) An import surplus is almost the same as a current account deficit (again subject to this small adjustment).

When a country has an export surplus, the demand exercised on its output by foreigners (i.e. exports) exceeds the domestic demand which spills outside the country (i.e. imports). For example, Japan has had an export surplus for many years. So, when exports exceed imports, there is a net addition to demand for domestic output. This net addition is one of the four elements of demand for domestic output (the others being consumer demand, investment demand and government demand for goods and services) which, together, determine the magnitude of domestic output. Hence, when exports go up due to an improvement of business conditions abroad, there will be a net increase in demand for domestic goods and services and a resulting increase in domestic output.

When a country has an import surplus, the domestic demand which spills outside the country (i.e. imports) exceeds the demand exercised on domestic output by foreigners (i.e. exports). For example, the U.S. has had an import surplus for a long time. So, when imports exceed exports, there is a net subtraction from demand for domestic output. This difference between imports and exports has to be subtracted from the sum of the three positive elements of demand for domestic output (consumer demand, investment demand, and government demand for goods and services) to get the total demand for domestic output. Hence, when there is a change in domestic tastes towards foreign produced goods (for example, VCR's) or an increased desire to spend vacations abroad, there will be an increase in imports of goods and services, with similar decrease in net demand for domestic goods and services, and a resulting decrease in domestic output.

One further point is worth noting. Our ability to understand and even predict international trade flows is far superior to our ability to understand and predict international capital flows. For example, we know that, when a currency gets cheaper (when it depreciates), the current account of that country will not improve immediately because the increase in exports and decrease in imports occur only with a time lag. (This is called the J effect.) Eventually, after this time lag, the current account will improve under nearly all circumstances. But – since capital flows heavily involve anticipations, and these are often ill understood and ill predictable – our ability to gauge the effect of various factors on these capital flows and, hence, on the exchange rate is very limited. This means that a lot of short term and medium term exchange rate fluctuations, which in turn ultimately affect exports and imports, thus national income, are far from fully understood.

It should also be noted that, on a world basis, exports should equal imports. (Actually, due to statistical problems, partially caused by various evasions, world import figures exceed world export figures substantially.) On a world basis, export surpluses also should equal import surpluses. Thus, for every import surplus, such as that of the U.S., there has to be an export surplus elsewhere. Conversely, for every export surplus, such as that of Japan, there has to be an import surplus elsewhere. (But, as noted above, the statistics are imperfect.)

Since we know that the three parts of the balance of payments for any country must sum to zero, any country's current account surplus (e.g. Japan) must be equal and opposite to the sum its private capital flows plus central bank intervention capital flows. So, the net capital outflow must equal its trade surplus. Conversely, any country's current account deficit (e.g. the U.S.) must be equal and opposite to the sum of its private capital flows and central bank intervention capital flows. So, the net capital inflow must equal its trade deficit.

On a world basis, capital exports must equal capital imports. Another name for a country's capital exports is foreign investment by that country. Another name for a country's capital imports is receipt of foreign investment from abroad. On a world basis, the sum of foreign investment by all countries must equal the sum of receipts of foreign investment by all countries. Japan has been the biggest foreign investor in recent years; the U.S. has been the biggest recipient of foreign investment.

There is also a relationship between a country's domestic savings and investment on the one hand and its foreign investment on the other.

For countries which have a current account surplus (i.e. net export surplus, also called net foreign investment), such as Japan, the following pertains: national savings (private sector savings minus public sector dissavings; also known as private sector savings minus the government deficit) equals its domestic investment plus its foreign investment.

For countries with a a current account deficit (i.e. net import surplus, also called receipt of foreign investment from other countries), such as the U.S., the following pertains: national savings (private sector savings minus public sector dissavings; also known as private sector savings minus the government deficit) plus the receipts of foreign investment (the import surplus) from other countries equals its domestic investment. Sometimes this is stated as: national savings plus foreign savings (since savings in other countries are the counterpart of receipts of foreign investment from other countries) equals domestic investment. Hence, for the U.S., with its import surplus, some of our domestic investment has its counterpart in savings done abroad by foreigners.

We may state the import of this chapter. Exchange rates are the result of a whole complex series of factors which derive from financial flows and trade flows. The exchange rates impact imports and exports. These, in turn, affect national income.

14. PRODUCTIVITY

Productivity has a long history. It first started increasing at a substantial pace in 18th century Britain. It has been increasing in a rising number of countries ever since, as these countries joined the Industrial Revolution.

Countries which started the industrialization process in more recent decades are capable of faster growth rates of productivity due to the vast backlog of technology waiting to be exploited by them. However, the realization of this potential requires substantial investment and substantial application of resources to education. Failure to do this means that productivity will grow at a slower pace or not at all, possibly even declining.

The most widely used concept of productivity is labor productivity, i.e. output per worker, or per work-hour. This is extremely important. The only way to achieve long run advances in general living standards is to increase labor productivity. And that, in turn, will increase over the decades only if the average ratio of the factors of production – capital, technology, education and land (including known natural resources) – to the factor of production, labor, increases.

Another concept is total factor productivity. Basically, this measures the efficiency with which the factors are used to produce output. Obviously, higher efficiency results in more output, lower efficiency in less output. But, the scope for increasing the efficiency of production is often limited. Sometimes it can be fairly substantial, for example in the transition in China after the death of Mao in 1976.

Unfortunately, productivity can be very hard to measure. This is particularly true in modern times. Years ago, for example, the number of pig iron ingots per week could be counted easily. But now, services dominate in industrialized countries. And services are notoriously hard to measure in quantitative terms. How, for example, can we count the output of teachers, engineers, musicians, clerks, etc.?

To make matters worse, rapid technological change presents practically insurmountable difficulties in counting real output, hence efficiency in production. As a result, when measuring productivity changes in industries with rapid technological change, there is a certain arbitrariness in the measurements.

In the U.S., for example, a well respected team of economists concluded in the mid 90's that measures of inflation (rate of price increase) were overstated by around one per cent. This meant that measures of real output increases were understated by about the same proportion. Hence, productivity growth similarly was also understated.

These types of measurement problems tend to dog all industrialized countries, since all are heavily into services and all are likely to be involved in at least some significant industries undergoing rapid technological change. So, the measured rates of productivity growth will always be under somewhat of a cloud.

Productivity advances also change over time. For example, productivity increases in the US were high after World War II until the early '70s. Then, productivity increases dropped greatly until the mid '90s. Thereafter, productivity growth once again rose substantially.

15. INCENTIVES

Incentives are important in economics. This has been known for more than two hundred years; it was known at the time of Adam Smith, indeed probably long before. But, the last couple of decades have seen a rediscovery of the significance of incentives, usually presented under the heading of supply-side economics.

The basic idea is this. If incentives to work can be raised, more people will work, they will be more productive and more will work longer hours; as a result, output will rise faster. Similarly, if business incentives to invest in plant, equipment, buildings, etc. can be raised, the stock of capital will grow faster (as will the stock of technology) and so will raise output. This then led to exploration of ways to increase incentives in order to increase the supply of output.

The basic incentive to work is the pay received as a result of work. Similarly, the basic incentive to invest is the net profit expected as a result of the investment. Tax policy can change these incentives, hence change the supply of output.

A reduction in payroll taxes, such as Social Security taxes, for example, will increase the after-tax receipts of workers, thus increase their incentive to work. It will also increase the employer incentive to hire, since each person hired is now less expensive. In many countries in Western Europe the payroll taxes are so high that employers don't want to hire. This is an important reason for the high, double digit unemployment rates in many of these countries. At the same time, high personal income taxes also reduce the after-tax income from work, exercising a negative work incentive effect.

Similarly, an increase in permitted depreciation allowances (which reduces taxes on corporations) has the effect of increasing the incentive to invest, thus increasing the amount of the factor of production, capital, and hence output.

There are many other incentives. One that has secured a lot of attention is the incentive to raise prices and wages. Expected future inflation creates such incentive. This may be observed in very poignant form in situations where sudden, huge drops in a country's exchange rate result in great expected subsequent price rises for imported goods in terms of that country's currency, thus creating pressure for price and wage rises. This occurred in an exacerbated form in some Asian countries in 1998 and in Argentina in 2002.

A decrease in the personal income tax increases the incentive to purchase goods and services, since households are left with greater after-tax income. A decrease in tariffs increases the incentive to import from abroad, since imports will be less expensive. A decrease in welfare payments increases the incentive to work, since the welfare recipient will now be in need of more monetary receipts from sources other than welfare. Something like this appears to have happened in the U.S. in the mid to late 1990's. An increase in subsidies for having large families can affect the number of children and the size of the population. This effect is probably significant if the subsidies are very large for large families, as in the Canadian province of Quebec. Tax policy which greatly reduces the after-tax income of skilled workers can eventually result in skill shortages. This has happened in Northern Europe. Good business conditions provide incentive to immigrate. University financial aid programs promote the incentive to remain in college, hence increase the stock of education.

One subject of much contention has been the incentive to save. Savings are the obverse side of consumption, since after-tax household income is either saved or consumed. It appears that the principal incentive is through consumption. In other words, people consume based on their income and the incentives to consume. Savings are what's left over. However, there have been attempts to stimulate savings by elimination of taxes on interest receipts in certain types of savings accounts. Results seem questionable, at least for the interest rates and tax rates found in the U.S.

Some incentives are quite strong, others very weak or practically nonexistent. This is a matter of behavior. So, each incentive should be analyzed in detail before any policy considerations are addressed.

16. EXPECTATIONS

Expectations (or anticipations) of the future are very important because they affect behavior in the present, For example, expectations of future business conditions will affect business behavior right now.

Expectations are important in many, varied economic areas including investment, consumption, wage rise demands, international financial capital movements, exchange rates, etc.

Investment in plant, capital equipment, and commercial buildings is undertaken when expected future profitability exceeds the cost of financing. But expected future profitability in turn depends on expected future cash flows. These cash flows are not facts, but expectations. So, current business investment depends on what business thinks will happen in the future. An expected future recession will tend to reduce current investment, hence aggregate demand. This will tend to bring on the very recession which is anticipated.

Household consumption depends mostly on current income. However, expectations of the future – particularly when very different from the present – can affect consumption right now. For example, an anticipated severe recession will have the effect of causing at least some consumption slowdown as people fear job losses. This then actually helps to bring on the recession.

Expectations are also important in the process of inflation. Expected inflation causes wage rise demands which, in turn, cause future inflation. In the U.S. the "built-in" rate of inflation in the latter 80's and most of the 90's was in the 3 per cent range. That was the inflation rate anticipated by the public based on years of experience. In countries where inflation has been high for many years, expectations of future inflation are also likely to be very high. And such expectations are difficult to change.

The markets for valuation of financial assets are particularly susceptible to expectations of the future. These markets include the stock market, the real estate market, the bond market, and the gold market. History has shown that there can be tremendous fluctuations in the valuation of assets, much of which depends on expectations of the future economy, future profitability, future inflation, future tax laws and other future phenomena.

Exchange rates are also dependent on expectations of the future. For example, if a country's asset markets (stock, bond, real estate) are expected to rise above average, financial flows are likely to go into that country, increasing its current (spot) exchange rate. International financial flows (or, capital movements) are huge in today's world and heavily dependent on expectations.

Economists have ways of classifying expectations. In particular, the notion of adaptive expectations was popular at one time. This held that trends in the more or less recent past are the principal explanation of the expected future. So, if the inflation rate was 10 per cent in the recent past, the idea of adaptive expectations held that it was likely to be around 10 per cent in the near future.

This somewhat rigid approach to expectations was replaced by the concept of rational expectations, which held that people are basically rational, hence take into account all relevant factors in their anticipations of the future. For example, if the inflation rate was 10 per cent in the recent past, but the government came in with a credible anti-inflation plan, then the expected rate of inflation in the near future would be less than 10 per cent.

Rational expectations also holds that people don't make the same errors over and over again, since they learn from experience. For example, if economic policy announcements by the government turn out to be incorrect or ineffectual, the public will eventually pay no attention to them.

In summary, expectations are very important. But our knowledge of how they are formed is quite imperfect.

17. LAGS

The existence of lags has a significant impact on the economy. A lag exists whenever there is a time interval between a cause and its effects. Some lags are so short that the effect is practically instantaneous. Others are as long as a year ort even longer. In some cases, the effect comes at a particular moment of time. In other instances, the lag is a distributed lag, so that the effects appear over a period of time.

Basically, financial markets react very quickly to information. Real markets in the economy react far, far more slowly. So, lags tend to be extremely short in financial markets such as the stock market. Lags tend to be extensive in real markets, such as the labor market.

In the financial or asset markets, anything that impinges on the market will have an immediate effect, often in seconds. These financial markets include the stock market, the money market (for short term financial obligations and the short term interest rate), the bond market (for long term financial obligations), the mortgage market (for mortgage obligations), the foreign exchange market and the real estate market. Of these, the real estate market has somewhat longer lags; the others have extremely short lags, i.e. almost instantaneous reactions. So, a new piece of news on a company will instantly affect its stock price. A new action by the Fed will instantly affect the short term interest rate. A new development on inflation will instantly affect the short term and possibly the long term interest rates.

In the real markets, in contrast to the financial markets, lags are everywhere. And, they can be extensive. Real markets include: the retail markets for consumer goods and services; the wholesale markets for consumer goods and services; the markets for industrial goods and services; the labor markets; the rental and leasing markets; the markets for technology; the markets for education; the import and exports markets for goods and services.

In all these markets, lags are important; these lags vitally affect the way the economy behaves. When there is an increase in investment, the resulting increase in national income takes time. When there is an increase in exports, the resulting increase in national income takes time. When there is an increase in government expenditure, the resulting increase in national income takes time. All of these demonstrate the principle of the multiplier (the amount by which an initial increase in demand is multiplied to get the final increase in national income). So, the operation of the multiplier principle is not instantaneous; it takes time.

When inflation speeds up unexpectedly, it takes time for labor to adjust wages in both union and individual wage bargaining sessions. This lag itself substantially affects how the inflationary process operates. The results for the economy would be quite different if wage adjustment to inflation operated instantaneously. Indeed, any difference between expected inflation and the subsequent actual inflation engenders further changes in inflation. If there were no lags, the actual and expected inflation would be equal

When the exchange rate depreciates, improvement in the trade balance (exports minus imports) takes time. In fact, there is a well known short run effect of exchange rate depreciation, the J effect. This effect shows that the initial result of an exchange rate depreciation is a deterioration of the trade balance, rather than an improvement. It is only after exporters (selling to foreign importers) and importers (buying from abroad) have had time to adjust to the new exchange rate that an improvement occurs in the trade balance. This usually takes a few months.

So, lags are important in economics. In general, if the initial and final points of an economic sequence are known, then there is a time series process of intermediate points between them in all real markets. There is no instantaneous leap from beginning to end.

18. WAGE/PRICE FLEXIBILITY

Wage/price flexibility refers to the response of wages relative to changes in prices (inflation). It is important because economies with high wage/price flexibility behave differently from those with low wage/price flexibility.

With a steady rate of inflation, wages eventually anticipate the inflation; so, wages and prices will go up more or less together, if there is no productivity change. This means that real wages (wages divided by prices) remain the same. (If productivity rises, then wages will rise faster than the price inflation, and real wages will go up.)

If inflation speeds up, wage rises lag behind price rises, since the higher inflation is not fully anticipated. The wage bargaining process takes time. Union wage bargaining contracts tend to be two or three years in length. Individual salary reviews tend to be annual. In the meantime, wages and salaries lag behind price rises. This means that real wages go down somewhat, if there is no productivity increase. (If productivity does rise, then real wages go up with the rise in productivity but down due to the inflation effect, making the net outcome uncertain.)

If the shoe is on the other foot and inflation slows down, wage rises will tend to be ahead of the now smaller price rises, since the lower inflation is not fully anticipated. In this case, the time taken by the wage bargaining process works in favor of labor. This means that real wages go up somewhat. (If productivity rises, this produces an additional factor for rise in real wages.)

As a practical matter, wage flexibility is greater upwards than downwards. There is tremendous resistance to an actual decline in money wages and usually at least some resistance even to a decline in the rate of increase of money wages.

So, when price inflation unexpectedly drops due to a decline in demand, the result is not only an impact on wage inflation but also an impact on real national output. These two effects are called a price effect (a price/wage/inflation effect) and a real effect (a real output/employment/unemployment effect). The drop in price inflation will cause a decline in wage inflation – with a lag – but in less than proportion to the drop in price inflation. It will also result in a drop in real national output and rise in the unemployment rate. (Eventually – with the passage of enough time – the wage inflation will adjust to the new, lower price inflation.)

If the real world were different, i.e. if wage response to price changes were full and instantaneous, the economy would behave differently. Price inflation and wage inflation then would go down simultaneously and – importantly – real national output and unemployment would not be affected at all.

When price inflation unexpectedly goes up due to an increase in demand, wage flexibility is likely to be greater. But the result will again be not only an impact on wage inflation but also an impact on real national output. The rise in price inflation will cause a rise in wage inflation - with a lag – but somewhat less than in proportion to the rise in price inflation. It will also result in a rise in national output and fall in the unemployment rate. (Eventually, with the passage of enough time – the wage inflation will adjust to the higher price inflation.) (For extremely high price inflation rates, wage inflation may jump ahead of price inflation.)

So far we have dealt with the flexibility of money wages relative to prices. This relationship determines the real wage. What happens when the real wage is set too high? This could happen, for example, with a very high minimum wage, as is true in some European countries. Or it could happen if payroll taxes are very high, as they are in some European countries. In effect it makes the real wage, as seen from the employer's viewpoint, very high.

Under such conditions – with mandated high real wages – the result will be a very high unemployment rate. This was true in some European countries in the 'nineties. When labor is made very, very expensive for employers, these employers simply don't want to hire such workers, particularly if it is difficult and expensive – for legal reasons – to get rid of such workers later. (Of course, the state has to support the resulting unemployed with costly unemployment compensation and welfare programs.)

These rigidities have grown up in tandem with expensive welfare states which have to be financed. So, high payroll taxes (and other taxes) are needed to finance the expensive social programs. In turn the high payroll taxes create high unemployment rates which then lead to expensive social programs for those without work, which, in turn, have to be financed with high taxes. These countries have found it extremely difficult to escape from this vicious circle.

What happens when real wages in a country have to be reduced? This may be necessary, for example, because the exchange rate has gone up, making the country's products too expensive in foreign markets. Or it may be that new, less expensive technology elsewhere has put downward pressure on product prices, making it essential to reduce wages.

Direct attempts to cut real wages by cutting money wages may be very difficult. In Britain, in the mid-twenties, the attempt to cut the money wages of coal miners to save foreign markets for British coal, which had become too expensive as a result of a substantial rise in the value of the British pound, led to a major coal miners' strike which turned into a disastrous general strike (the only one ever in the country).

It is easier by far to reduce real wages when there is some inflation, by the much simpler expedient of keeping money wages constant while prices go up. The psychology is just different. There is less perception of real wage decline and less resistance when prices go up than when money wages go down.

19. INDUSTRY STRUCTURE

Industry structure is important in macroeconomics because it determines the way in which pricing decisions are made. It also affects time lags.

There are four types of industry structure: perfect competition, monopolistic (or imperfect) competition; oligopoly; monopoly. Of these, monopolistic competition and oligopoly encompass the vast majority of all industries. Perfect competition is relatively rare outside some agricultural products. Monopoly has been largely confined to some regulated industries.

Many economists build their theories of macroeconomics on the implicit assumption that perfect competition is the dominant market structure. Unfortunately, this is quite unrealistic in the modern world.

Perfect competition is an industry structure where all firms are small, all produce completely identical products, entry and exit in the industry are very easy, no firm has any control at all over the price it can charge for its output since the price is completely market determined, and each firm can sell as much as it wishes. Under these circumstances, each firm simply sells at the market determined price and produces output until the point where the additional cost incurred in producing the last unit equals the market price.

The mere description of perfect competition indicates its unreality in the world. The vast majority of firms do not produce identical output and they are certainly not all small. Perfect competition is, of course, found under some conditions, for example, production of a specific kind of wheat by many farms, each small relative to the total size of that market. But these instances comprise only a tiny part of the total economy.

Most of the output of goods and services in the economy is produced by industries which have the industry structure of monopolistic competition or oligopoly. In both of these, firms have some control over price. Within limits, they can charge a higher price and sell less, or a lower price and sell more.

Monopolistic competition is an industry structure where all firms are small, but they produce products which differ; entry and exit in the industry are very easy; and each firm has some control over the price it can charge for its output. Under these circumstances each firm must determine whether to charge more or to charge less. This type of market structure includes much of retail trade, most services, small manufacturing and other sectors. In principle, each firm produces output until the point where the additional cost incurred in producing the last unit equals the additional revenue it can get by selling the last unit. This will be less than the market price since more units of its particular product can be sold only by lowering the sales price for all units sold. In practice, due to the uncertainty and lack of knowledge of both the additional revenue and the additional cost of selling the last unit, a practical way of determining price is utilized.

Oligopoly is an industry structure where firms are large and relatively few in number, where each has a substantial market share, where entry and exit in the industry are difficult, where the products produced may be either identical or different, and each firm typically has a good deal of control over the price it can charge for its output. In principle, price and output determination can become very complex, since the actions of each firm affect the actions of every other firm in the industry. In practice, there is great uncertainty and lack of knowledge of potential action of the other firms in the industry. As a result, oligopolistic firms resort to practical ways of determining price.

Given the rarity of perfect competition, why do many economists try to build their macro analysis onto this type of market structure? There are several answers: it is the easiest market structure to analyze; it has the longest history and its analysis is best developed; it is somehow considered symbolic of the type of competition faced in the two largest industry structures.

In the real world of oligopoly and monopolistic competition, of uncertainty and lack of knowledge, the most common type of pricing behavior is markup pricing. In this pricing method, the business takes a major cost element – such as labor costs, material costs, or a combination of the two – and marks up the cost per unit of product by a factor which is sufficiently large to cover all the other business costs as well as profit, so as to yield an adequate expected average rate of profit over the good years and bad years of the business.

Markup ratios differ in different types of business. They are not the same in a supermarket than in a furniture store. But, regardless of the exact type of business, they are all designed to yield an adequate rate of return over the years.

From these markups, we may determine the average rate of markup for the economy. If this markup is higher, profits will have a larger share of national income. If the markup is less, profits will have a lower share of national income. So, the average rate of markup is closely related to income distribution.

Industry structure is also related to time lags. In perfect competition, a change in costs will affect prices and output very rapidly. But in oligopoly, a change in costs may have little or no immediate effect since prices, once set, are not changed every day or even every quarter. The same may be said, to a lesser extent, of monopolistic competition.

This means that, on the average for the economy as a whole, a change in costs is translated into a change in prices only with a time lag. This follows a well known principle: real markets adjust slowly.

20. UNCERTAINTY

Uncertainty is a fact of life in economics. We live in a world of uncertainty. No one knows with precision what the future will bear.

This lack of certainty has very significant effects on economic behavior and on the economy. It affects the amount of investment undertaken by business, the amount of consumption by households, the valuation placed on assets in the asset markets and labor market behavior in terms of wage push.

Basically, there is a discount placed on uncertainty. We would rather have a definite dollar next year than an equal chance at two dollars and no dollars at all. In other words, it is not only the average, or expected, value of possible outcomes that counts, but the degree of uncertainty that attached to the expected outcome. So, uncertainty acts to reduce investment, reduce consumption, and reduce valuation of assets. Uncertainty in job security acts to reduce wage rise demands.

When business considers investment in plant, equipment and residential and commercial buildings, it must consider not only the expected rate of return from these investments, but also the degree of uncertainty, i.e. the risk, attached to the expected returns. There is a very simple principle involved: the greater the risk, the greater will have to be the returns to make an investment worthwhile. So, in times of great uncertainty, business will cut back on investment everywhere.

Consumption is also affected somewhat by uncertainty, though much less so than investment. In times of great uncertainty, with doubts about job retention, households cut back consumption, particularly durables. This was the case, for example, in some Asian countries, after the foreign exchange debacle in the latter 1990's.

Asset market valuations – such as the stock market, the real estate market, the bond market – tend to be greatly affected by uncertainty. Basically, uncertainty reduces asset market valuations, since the financial community places a discount on uncertainty. So, when the outlook seems to be clear and favorable, price/earnings ratios in the stock market will be high. When the outlook is unclear and less favorable, price/ earnings ratios will be much lower. In the bond market, when there is much uncertainty about the possible extent of future inflation, the price of bonds will be lower since the possibility of inflation requires a higher discount of future cash flows.

Labor market behavior also depends on uncertainty. Job retention uncertainty causes union bargaining to put job security high up on their list of demands, with wage increases further down. The same phenomenon may be observed in non-union, individual employee salary review sessions. When such job retention uncertainty diminishes, wage demands will move up towards the top of bargaining session demands, so that upward wage push becomes more important.

Technological change is an important special factor. It produces a great deal of uncertainty. But this type of uncertainty has a different effect. Technological change means that the need for investment rises rather than falls, since new technology is usually incorporated in new capital goods. To fall behind is to lose out.

Finally, uncertainty becomes very important under conditions of very high inflation. Since such inflations themselves fluctuate greatly in their weekly and monthly rates, there is a huge amount of uncertainty attached to them. The result is that lenders demand extraordinarily high real interest rates to compensate them for the degree of risk they must bear as a result of the uncertainty. These conditions produce the highest real interest rates anywhere. In fact, lending may practically dry up almost completely due to unwillingness to lend in the face of such high risk.

21. INCOME DISTRIBUTION

Wage and salary payments take up the lions share of national income. In the US, these have been running at about two-thirds of total gross domestic product (or not far from eighty per cent of national income). Profits in the US take a far smaller proportion; gross profits (which include depreciation) typically fluctuate around one fifth of gross domestic product (or net profits around one tenth of national income).

We want to consider the following question: what determines the share of the national income that goes to profits? Clearly this has to do with the size of the average markup in the economy. If the markup is higher, profits will constitute a larger share of national income. If the markup is lower, profits will constitute a smaller share of national income.

Profits do vary as a proportion of total national income on a cyclical basis. This is true even if the average level of markup in the economy does not change.

At low levels of national income, with higher levels of unemployment, business profits are down because sales volume is down. At high levels of national income, with low levels of unemployment, business profits are up because sales volume is up. Profits go up and down proportionately faster than national income. In fact, at a low enough level of national income, profits can turn negative. So, profits will be a higher proportion of national income when national income is high at the top of a cycle and a lower proportion of national income when national income is low at the bottom of a cycle.

In addition, the average level of markup itself varies somewhat over the business cycle. When national income is lower and excess capacity higher, businesses tend to shade their price quotations somewhat. This is done in various ways. Some "firsts" are sold as "seconds", in effect reducing the price. More discounts appear. Quality improves without increase in price. The net effect is a reduction in markups.

When net income is higher and excess capacity shrinks to low levels, businesses tend to increase their price quotations. "Seconds" become "firsts", in effect increasing the price. Some discounts disappear. Quality improvements command price hikes. The net effect is an increase in markups.

So, these cyclical changes in the average markup amount to an additional factor impacting on profits, hence an additional factor explaining why profits vary as a percentage of national income over the cycle.

But, what about the very long run changes in markups and in profits as a proportion of national income over the decades?

Some societies are very dynamic. Their economies usually operate at high levels of demand, low excess capacity and low unemployment rates. Under these circumstances, over a long period of time, the pressure of demand will slowly tend to increase the average level of markups to such an extent that markups do not fall back completely to preceding lower levels when the economy undergoes a cyclical decline. The net effect, over the decades, is an increase in profits as a percentage of national income due to increase in the average level of markups.

Other societies are phlegmatic. Their economies more frequently operate at low levels of demand, high excess capacity and high unemployment rates. Under these circumstances, over a long period of time, the deficit in demand will slowly tend to decrease the average level of markups to such an extent that it is reduced at all levels of the cycle. The net effect, over the decades, is a decrease in profits as a percentage of national income due to decrease in the average level of markups.

There are many other aspects of income distribution which are more the subject of microeconomics than macroeconomics, though both may come into play. For example, there has been a decline in the income of unskilled workers relative to skilled workers in recent decades in the US. The causes are two. Technological change requires employees who have more skills than was true years ago, while there are fewer jobs for the unskilled. This, combined with a shortage of personnel in many skilled areas and a surplus in the unskilled sector, means higher incomes for the former and lower incomes for the latter.

In addition to this dominant factor, the internationalization of trade has shifted some employment opportunities of the unskilled and the low skilled out of the industrialized countries into the underdeveloped world. As a result, unskilled workers in the industrialized countries have seen a further erosion of job opportunities.

Another income distribution phenomenon has to do with the substantial entry of women into the labor force, increasingly in many types of work formerly almost entirely staffed by men. Since there is a tendency for high earning men and high earning women to marry each other, this phenomenon tends to make the family income distribution more unequal than formerly was the case.

So, micro factors as well as macro factors may be very significant in analysis of income distribution among income classes and among industries.

Income distribution has many implications, particularly on consumption. For example, luxury goods, extensive travel and the like are favorably impacted by a skew income distribution.

However, total consumption in a country will tend to be higher if income distribution is less unequal. High income recipients and heavy profit recipients tend to save a larger proportion, and consume a lesser proportion, of their income than low income recipients. And high income recipients own a much greater share of the country's assets than just their numbers would indicate; hence they receive a much greater share of profits and capital gains. As a result, most of the country's household savings are made by the higher income groups and very little by low income groups. So, since low income recipients consume a higher proportion of their income than higher income recipients, a more equal income distribution tends to increase total consumption.

22. ECONOMIC GROWTH

Economic growth occurs when output grows faster than population (see: chapters 5,6). There are only about 25-30 countries that have already achieved high living standards through long term sustained growth. The rest of the 200 or so countries in the world have not yet reached these levels.

High living standards require high ratios of capital, education and land (natural resources) relative to labor. But, due to the law of diminishing returns, these high ratios to labor by themselves are not sufficient for long term sustained economic growth. Eventually, further increase in these factors relative to labor will result in smaller and smaller increments of output.

What is needed is technological change. There is old technology and new technology. Old technology is that which already exists. New technology is newly created every day.

The law of diminishing returns applies to old technology. When more and more of the same old technology is applied to labor, raising the ratio of old technology to labor, eventually equal increments of such technology produce lesser and lesser increments of output.

New technology is continuously different. So, each increment of new technology applied to labor, and to the other factors of production, will create more output, forever. The law of diminishing returns will not apply, since – by definition and by observation – it applies only when more and more of the same factor is added. So, increments of new technology, in principle, can yield increasing returns, constant returns or diminishing returns. It all depends on the particular new technology.

The advanced, industrialized, high living standard countries, largely at the edge of the world technological frontier, need new technology, i.e. technological progress to have economic growth.

The rest of the world, far back from the world technological frontier, can experience economic growth using the existing supply of old technology. These countries are not dependent on the technological progress of new technology for economic growth

23. CONVERGENCE

Anyone who has traveled in the U.S., Canada, Western Europe, Australia and New Zealand, and Japan will have observed the similarity in living standards. To be sure, all of these countries have differences, some more substantial than others, but all are broadly similar in average living standards as commonly measured. A further look elicits the observation that they use much the same technology, tend to have similar educational attainments and broadly similar ratios of capital to labor.

Further travel, with repeat visits over a decade or two, in countries such as Singapore, Israel and South Korea quickly shows that such countries have greatly increased their living standards and seem to be well on the way towards convergence in living standards to those of the most advanced countries. But...still further travel, with repeat visits over a decade or two, to many other countries reveals that living standards have been low and remain low, in some cases even declining further, with no visible convergence towards the high living standards of the successful countries.

So, this question arises: why is there convergence towards high living standards for some countries, but not for others.

There are some obvious reasons. Countries which have poorly developed legal systems, inadequate property rights, lack of personal safety, arbitrary government power, confiscation of property without adequate compensation, frequent serious disturbances including civil war, enormous endemic corruption, and other factors destructive of economic development are unlikely to get very far. But, there is much more to the subject of convergence.

There is a vast amount of technology in the world that is available to poor countries. (The rich countries have already largely utilized this technology.) But, since most technology is incorporated in capital goods, the poorer countries can only take advantage of this existing technology if they are able to increase the factor of production, capital, in their countries.

In addition, many poorer countries have a rather substantial excess labor supply - and in some cases even an excess of (poorly) educated labor - that cannot be employed because of an inadequate supply of the factor of production, capital.

A country will be on the way towards convergence (which will take decades) only if it can put aside a sufficient amount of its national output (plus any financial inflow from abroad) to increase the ratio of factors of production other than labor to the factor of production, labor, by reasonable amounts

This means a high rate of savings (which permits increase in the capital stock, and thereby in technology), a high rate of expenditure on the right kinds of education (which increases the stock of education incorporated in human beings), a high rate of exploration for natural resources (increasing the factor of production, land) and – also – a lowering of the rate of population growth (which makes it easier to increase the ratio of factors of production other than labor to the factor of production, labor). The education is necessary to run the technology.

The problem for the poorer countries is this: being poorer, it is much harder to put aside a relatively large share of their national output to provide for the necessary future growth. It is harder to have a high savings rate, harder to provide for a high rate of educational expenditures, harder to have extensive exploration for natural resources. It is also often harder to reduce the population growth rate, since children may provide the only social safety net and the only retirement pension, since the state cannot afford this role.

The result is this. Those countries which can meet the goal of setting aside sufficient output from the national product are on the way to convergence, a lengthy process that takes decades. Some will meet success faster, others more slowly.

Other countries do not meet the goal of setting aside sufficient output from their national product to allow convergence. These countries will often show divergence, i.e. an increasing gap between their living standards and those of the advanced countries.

24. BUSINESS FLUCTUATIONS

Business fluctuations have been studied for more than a century. Observations indicated a certain degree of regularity in the ups and downs of business; hence, these fluctuations came to be known as, "business cycles".

Business cycles consist of four phases – troughs, expansions, peaks and contractions. Generally, expansions are longer than contractions. So, there is growth of the economy over time. The length of expansions and contractions can vary considerably. Expansions, for example, can be as short as a year or can approach a decade in length. The same can be said of contractions. The amplitude of different cycles also varies considerably. Some, the Great Depression of the 1930's in particular, are very big; others are barely visible. Historically, the average length of a complete business cycle has been around five years, but in the 1980's and '90's the US cycle was about twice as long.

In the US, the business cycle is dated by a private body, the National Bureau of Economic Affairs, rather than by the government. Usually, this dating occurs a considerable time after the fact, since statistics run late and are revised subsequently, and all this has to be interpreted. So, an upturn may be well under way before it is announced that the trough has ended.

There have been many theories of the business cycle over more than a century. We shall subsume them under three approaches which seem to hold the field today: theories which depend on fluctuations in aggregate demand, i.e. the economy's total demand for goods and services; theories which depend on fluctuations in aggregate, or total, supply;

and theories which depend on changes in the growth rate of the money supply and, hence, in interest rates.

Aggregate demand theories depend on fluctuations in total demand for goods and services produced by the economy and in fluctuations in demand for the major components of total demand. Since there are four components – consumer demand, investment demand, government demand and net export demand (or minus net import demand) – any or all of these may be the most significant causal element in a business cycle.

Demand for investment is exercised by business. It is known to fluctuate proportionately more than consumer demand. Business firms undertake investment projects depending on the expected rate of return from these projects relative to the cost of financing, which in turn is related to the rate of interest. The expected rate of return depends on the outlook for the future. So, changes in business expectations and confidence can affect demand for investment greatly.

Investment demand, in turn, can be broken down into demand for new and replacement plant and equipment, demand for housing and demand for increase in inventories (which can be a minus quantity). So, any change in demand for these subcomponents, which depends on the business outlook, will affect business fluctuations.

The second, and largest, element of total demand, demand for consumer goods and services, is exercised by households. This will be affected, to at least some degree, by consumer confidence. There are three subcomponents of consumer demand – non-durable goods, durable goods and services. Of these, durable goods such as automobiles, are most affected by consumer confidence and fluctuate the most during the business cycle.

Consumer demand is also affected by government policies in regard to taxes and transfer payments. Tax increases will reduce, and tax decreases increase, household income. Similarly, increases in transfer payments will increase, while decreases in transfer payments decrease, household income. So, changes in government policies – called fiscal policies – which change household income will indirectly change consumer demand.

The third element of total demand is government demand for goods and services, including both Federal Government and State and Local Governments. This is affected by Federal Government fiscal policy on outlays for goods and services. Fluctuations in fiscal policy can cause fluctuations in business conditions

Finally, the fourth element of total demand is net demand from other countries. This is positive if the country has an export surplus, or negative if the country has an import surplus. Fluctuations in the net demand by foreign countries also impact fluctuations in the economy.

So, fluctuations in these four elements of demand are vital in explaining the business cycle's fluctuations in demand. They are particularly important in explaining the business cycle peak and trough.

Real business cycle theories depend on fluctuations in supply. Random real shocks can create business cycles. Such shocks include technological changes, drastic changes in oil supply, major prolonged labor strikes, the effect of tax changes on supply, productivity shocks, and other factors which impact supply.

A negative supply shock, for example, such as the oil shocks of 1974 and 1979/80, can increase prices and decrease real incomes, thus reducing consumer demand and investment demand, causing the economy to fall into recession.

In contrast, a positive supply shock, such as the productivity increase created by some types of technological change, can cause an increase in investment and an upswing in the business cycle.

So, shocks which affect supply can create business cycles.

Monetary business cycle theories depend on fluctuations in the growth rate of the money supply. Monetarists focus on the changes in economic activity which result from increases or decreases in the growth rate of the money supply, which then affect interest rates.

A rise in the growth rate of the money supply, for example, will decrease interest rates; this decreases the cost of financing investment, hence increases the amount of investment. It will also tend to increase consumption, particularly durable goods. Moreover, a government induced decline in the interest rate, under some conditions, may be taken as a signal of enhanced future economic prospects and expected rates of return, further increasing investment.

A fall in the growth rate of the money supply will increase interest rates which increases the cost of financing investment, hence decreasing the amount of investment. It is often interpreted as action by the monetary authorities, the Fed in the US, to stop a business expansion before it creates too much inflation. Monetarists point to several business cycle upswings which were stopped through monetary action. A major example is the double business cycle of the early 1980's.

In practice, all three types of business cycle theories have much to contribute to understanding business fluctuations. It is, in fact, obvious that there have been demand fluctuations, supply fluctuations and monetary fluctuations in various combinations in the different business cycles over the decades.

In addition, we have to recognize that the relative size of industries that make up the economy has changed greatly over the years. Today, information processing and high tech have become much larger, so they comprise a noticeable part of the economy. As a result, factors which affect these industries are much more important. And, as these industries have become larger, fluctuations in demand for and supply of these industries have taken a much more prominent role in business fluctuations. In the latter nineteenth century, railroads and railroad construction were dominant. Later, it was steel and autos. Today, there has been an increasing shift to information processing and high technology; these will expand further in the foreseeable future.

25. DEMOGRAPHICS

Demography analyzes the population and its components. This includes population size, birth and death rates, population growth rates, age distribution, labor force size, male and female labor force participation rates, immigration and emigration, male/female ratios of different ages, and other aspects of the population.

All macroeconomic analysis has to distinguish between GDP growth rates on the one hand and GDP per capita growth rates on the other. These are the same only if the population growth rate is zero.

Generally, in the underdeveloped world, population growth rates are likely to be substantial, so that the per capita growth rate is quite a bit less than the GDP growth rate. Indeed, the per capita growth rate may even be negative, indicating declining living standards.

In contrast, in the industrialized countries, population growth rates tend to be low, or even negative, the latter indicating a declining population, e.g. Italy today. As a result, the difference between the GDP growth rate and the GDP per capita growth rate in the industrialized countries is likely to be low. And, for countries with declining population, the per capita growth rate is in fact greater than the GDP growth rate.

There are also very great differences between the industrialized countries and the underdeveloped countries in age structure of the population.

In the underdeveloped countries, with their much higher growth rates in population, the age distribution is skewed towards youth. This means that a large proportion of the population is too young to be in the regular labor force. On the other hand, only a small proportion of the population is retired. So, these societies have to support many non-working young, but relatively few non-working old. It also means that they should invest a substantial portion of their GDP in education, but will find it difficult or impossible to free sufficient resources to accomplish that goal.

In the industrialized nations, with their low or even negative growth rates of population, and greater survival rates, the age distribution is skewed towards old age. This means that a substantial proportion of the population is retired from the labor force. So, these societies have to support many non-working old. On the other hand, they have to support and provide education for a smaller proportion of the population which is young. However, due to the educational requirements of running a modern complex industrialized country, the educational needs for each person are far higher.

When all is said and done, the ratio which summarizes many of the problems of the industrialized countries is the ratio of those working to those not working. This ratio has been declining in these countries for years. So, a smaller and smaller number of workers have to support a larger and larger number of non-workers, especially the retired, who are living longer and longer.

In the underdeveloped countries, the inability to provide adequate education to many of the young results in low average educational attainments and substantial functional illiteracy rates. It also leads to large numbers of such economically marginally people eking out an existence in the service trades. This can be amply observed in South Asia and elsewhere.

In many of the industrialized countries, the need to provide pensions and medical benefits for the large numbers of the old results in high tax rates on employers which tends to discourage hiring and leads to high unemployment rates.

In recent years, economists have tried to analyze the problems of maintaining a large retired, non-working population in the industrialized countries. This has been studied through "generational accounting".

Historically, most of the government pension plans have been on a pay-as-you-go basis. This means that today's working population supports, through taxes, today's retired population. Later on, tomorrow's working population will in turn support today's working population once it reaches retirement years. Since the ratio of those who are retired to those who are working is declining, and taxes on today's working population are not sufficient, taxes on tomorrow's workers will have to be increased, perhaps to quite high levels. "Generational accounting" attempts to calculate the extent of this burden.

In all countries, the demographics of the population have substantial effects on the macro economy. The demand for housing, for example, is substantially affected by population growth rates. It is also affected by the size of household units. So, in industrialized countries, with their low population growth rates or negative population growth rates, demand for housing is adversely impacted. But this may be offset to a greater or lesser degree by the shrinkage in the size, and expansion in the numbers, of household units which is typically found under such conditions. There will also be a shift from larger to smaller dwelling units. Real estate prices and the valuation of dwelling units in the real estate market – an important asset market – tend to diminish.

Household saving is another important area affected by the age distribution of the population. This has been studied in the life cycle analysis of household consumption and savings, i.e. the effect of age on household savings. Those who are retired tend to dissave, i.e. consume more than their income. So, for the industrialized countries, a rise in the proportion of the population which is retired is likely to have a negative impact on household savings, which in turn affects the economy in a great many ways.

26. ASSET MARKETS

The financial markets for valuation of assets have become increasingly important in the world.

The big asset markets are: the stock market; the bond market; the short term money market; the real estate market. In addition there is a huge special international market, the foreign exchange market.

These financial markets determine the value of the various assets; most of these assets can fluctuate substantially in value. These fluctuations, in turn, can have important effects on the economy.

Household consumption depends mainly on current income, but to some extent also on household wealth. When the stock market goes up, household wealth increases. When it goes down, household wealth diminishes. The same principle applies to the other domestic asset markets. It has been found that each dollar change in household wealth results in a change of about two to five cents in consumer purchases. So, a high valuation of assets is favorable for the economy while a low valuation is unfavorable.

Business investment also is affected by the valuation of assets. When a corporation wants to spend money to buy plant or equipment, it has two broad alternatives. Either it can purchase the plant and equipment newly constructed or it can buy an existing firm which already owns the desired plant and equipment. When the stock market is high, i.e. when the ratio of market value to replacement cost is high, it becomes very expensive to buy another firm for cash. It is much cheaper to construct the desired plant and produce the desired equipment directly. This means that high stock market valuations are favorable for investment. Conversely, when the stock market is low, it becomes cheaper to buy another firm for cash. So, low stock market valuations are unfavorable for investment. Similarly for the real estate market.

In addition, high bond market valuations indicate low long term real interest rates. This means a lower financing cost for investment, which is favorable for investment.

The state of the asset markets also is important in determining the international flow of financial capital, hence foreign exchange rates. When the stock market is expected to rise, when the bond market is expected to rise, when the real estate market is expected to rise, these asset markets attract foreign financial capital wishing to participate in the expected rise. As a result, demand for that country's currency will rise and so will its exchange rate. Conversely, if these asset markets are expected to fall, foreigners will sell and convert back to their home currency, thus causing the exchange rate of the country to deteriorate.

As noted earlier, most asset markets can vary greatly in valuation. Of course, there is always uncertainty. The greater the uncertainty, the lower will be the valuation of an asset market. This follows an important principle: the greater the risk, the greater the return. This principle may also be stated as follows: the greater the uncertainty, the less is the capital valuation placed on each dollar of earnings. To put it briefly, a high degree of confidence in the future results in high asset valuations; a low degree of confidence in the future results in low asset valuations.

High stock market valuations are favorable for new business formations, since high market valuations make access to financial capital much easier. Those with money will be eager to buy into potentially successful fledgling companies which are expected to have subsequent public issues at high stock prices.

High stock market valuations, particularly rising stock market valuations, enhance government tax collections, as high capital gains taxes are collected when stocks are sold at large gains. This means that governments can reduce their deficits and even run a surplus,

But there are problems when stock market valuations and real estate market valuations become very high. This can lead to so-called "bubbles" which eventually burst, sending the economy downwards with the disinflation of these asset markets. In 1929, for example, it was said that the stock market was not only discounting the future, but the hereafter. A more recent example of a "bubble" was the Japanese real estate market and stock market in the later 1980's, running into the new century, which eventually had severe deleterious effects on the Japanese banking system and the Japanese economy, as both real estate market and stock market underwent disinflation. Another "bubble" was the US stock market in the late nineties, particularly the NASDAQ market. So, very high asset market valuations can lead to destabilization.

27. PLANNING HORIZONS

Planning horizons refer to the extent of the future considered in making present day decisions. A short planning horizon means that only the next few days or the next few months are considered in a decision made today. A long planning horizon means that the next few years, or even longer, are considered in making a decision today.

It is obvious that the nature of the decision has a lot to do with the length of the planning horizon. A corporation considering construction of a new plant necessarily must look some distance into the future. A hungry individual deciding whether to go to a restaurant clearly will have a rather short planning horizon.

The length of the planning horizon can affect business fluctuations, stock market fluctuations, purchases of consumer durables, business investment, housing investment and other economic phenomena.

Short planning horizons, which only take into account expected results in the very near future, tend to result in greater variability of consumer durables expenditures, business investment, housing construction, business fluctuations, and stock market values. Short planning horizons tend to create larger economic ups and downs.

Longer planning horizons, which take into account longer periods in the future, tend to result in much lesser variability in economic variables. By looking beyond expected short term ups and downs, longer term planning horizons tend to even out such ups and downs.

So, longer term planning horizons are very desirable. Given the amount of information available in today's world, it seems likely that planning horizons have in fact become somewhat longer.

28. CREATIVE DESTRUCTION

Economic progress does not proceed perfectly smoothly. New products replace old products, new industries replace old industries, new technologies old technologies.

The new advances; the old declines. The transistor replaced the vacuum tube, cellular phones replace standard phones, jet engines replaced propeller engines. In every case, there is a wrenching adjustment. Economic progress very often involves a new technology replacing an old technology, with a new industry replacing, in whole or in part, an old industry.

In the early days of a new product, a new industry, a new technology, at a certain stage prices will be high and profits substantial. The high prices, the innovations, the rosy projected outlook ease the financing of the industry. Then, as time goes on, prices decline but so do costs as volume expands. What we see is part of a product life cycle. Attainment of high volume, low costs, and adequate pricing means a profitable industry until competition brings down margins.

In the meantime, the old industry experiences lower and lower volume, price pressure and eventually losses instead of profits. The new industry has attracted resources which shift into the industry. The old industry experiences resource withdrawals. No one wants to put funds into such old industry.

This whole process has been called creative destruction and is associated with the work of Josef Schumpeter, an Austrian economist, later professor at Harvard.

29. POLICY: THE SHORT RUN AND THE LONG RUN

Government policies appropriate to the short run are often inappropriate for the long run.

The short run is a period short enough to reasonably assume that the quantities of the factors of production are unchanged. In the long run, the quantities of the factors of production grow or diminish.

Monetary policy, by its very nature, tends to be short run policy. The Fed controls short run nominal interest rates. These can vary substantially from one year to the next. The Fed influences, but does not control, long term nominal interest rates which are affected by expected inflation, risk and return characteristics, as well as other factors.

The major problems arise in fiscal policy. Here, good policies in the short run often are poor policies for the long run and vice-versa.

In a recession, for example, a good policy may require tax reductions and government expenditure increases in order to stimulate the economy through increase in aggregate demand. And...tax decreases have to be presented as "permanent", since it is well known that temporary tax reductions have a much lesser impact in boosting the economy than permanent tax reductions. But, all this is likely to create a substantial government deficit.

A few years down the line, when the economy has recovered, and when other conditions may well have changed – for example, the size of medical program costs and pension expenditures – continuation of the short run policy adopted at a time of recession becomes inappropriate. And so, there then have to be "permanent" tax increases and/or expenditure decreases. This, in fact, happened in the US in the 1980's.

The same principle applies in reverse to boom times when inflation threatens. This is a time to increase taxes "permanently" and reduce government expenditures in order to reduce aggregate demand. But...this short term policy becomes inappropriate a few years later when the economy is once again in recession and another set of "permanent" changes is required in taxes and government expenditures.

An obvious difficulty lies in the use of the concept, "permanent". The more people realize that "permanent" lasts only a few years, the less will such changes affect the economy and the more difficult it will be to use fiscal policy.

The contrast between the short run and the long run has been known for many years. No business will adopt short run policies and keep these unchanged forever. In that respect government is no different. But government is elephantine, lumbering and hard to move. So, changes come erratically at unspecified intervals. In the meantime, inappropriate policies - which once were appropriate – can continue much too long a time.

About the Author

Peter M. Gutmann is professor of Economics at Baruch College of the City University of New York.

He has a doctorate from Harvard University. His dissertation title was "Income Distribution, Asset Values and Economic Growth".

Professor Gutmann is widely known due to his pathbreaking work on the subterranean economy which created a whole industry of articles and books by economists from all over the world on that subject.

He is the author of "Macroeconomics in Brief". He has published in a range of economic journals including the American Economic Review, the Journal of Income Distribution, the Review of Economics and Statistics, and others.

Professor Gutmann teaches macroeconomics and growth economics at Baruch College of the City University of New York.